The New Testament

A Bibliography

The New Testament

A Bibliography

Daniel J. Harrington, S.J.

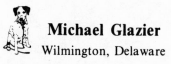

Michael Glazier
Wilmington, Delaware

BIOGRAPHICAL NOTE

Daniel J. Harrington, S.J., is professor of New Testament at Weston School of Theology in Cambridge, Massachusetts, and general editor of *New Testament Abstracts*. He earned his Ph.D. in Near Eastern Languages and Literatures at Harvard University in 1970. He is President of the Catholic Biblical Association (1985-86).

First published in 1985 by Michael Glazier, Inc., 1935 West Fourth Street. Wilmington, Delaware 19805.

Library of Congress Catalog Card Number **85-45447**
International Standard Book Number:
  The New Testament: A Bibliography 0-89435-535-8
Typography by Richard Reinsmith.
Cover design by Florence Bern.
Printed in the United States of America.

TABLE OF CONTENTS

Please Note

- We invite our readers to submit to the author any corrections, suggestions, or additions to the bibliography.
- An asterisk before a title indicates that the work is of broad interest and serves as a good introduction to the topic.

Introduction

When Michael Glazier sent to me the galleys of *The Church: A Bibliography* by Avery Dulles and Patrick Granfield, he suggested that I compile a similar bibliography for New Testament studies. His invitation coincided with my own desire to review and organize my work in the New Testament field, especially in connection with *New Testament Abstracts*. My first association with *New Testament Abstracts* was in the fall of 1962, and I have served as general editor since 1972. Over these years I have summarized thousands of books and articles. Preparation of this bibliography has provided me with the pleasant opportunity of reviewing all the issues of *New Testament Abstracts* since its inception in 1956 and of deciding what I now consider especially helpful and significant. I have also included some earlier publications.

The material contained in these bibliographical lists represents my perception of what should prove most useful for students, Christian educators, professional theologians, clergy, and interested laity. The lists have been prepared with English-speakers in mind, though I have included some foreign language items. An asterisk (*) before an entry indicates that the work is a good introduction to the topic. I have been ecumenical in choosing authors; some evangelicals may feel a bit slighted, however. I have followed the format established by Dulles and Granfield. My selection goes through 1984, with a sprinkling of 1985 titles.

My aim is to present an up-to-date and representative sample of the best books and articles available on a wide range of topics involved in the study of the New Testament. The topics under the heading "World of the New Testament" are so vast and complicated that I have generally restricted myself to translations of texts, bibliographies, methodological reflections, and syntheses.

Preparing this bibliography has been a happy exercise in remembering people and events from the past twenty-five years. I have often been conscious of my Jesuit brothers: John J. Collins, George W. MacRae, Stanley Marrow, and Simon Smith. I have thought frequently about those who have worked with me as managing editors on *New Testament Abstracts*: James W. Dunkly, Maurya P. Horgan, and Elizabeth G. Burr. To all these fine people, I dedicate this book in gratitude for their personal friendship and their dedication to *New Testament Abstracts*.

Daniel J. Harrington, S.J.
May 1985

I. Texts and Tools

1
Bibliographies

*Fitzmyer, J. A. *An Introductory Bibliography for the Study of Scripture.* Rev. ed. Rome: Biblical Institute Press, 1981.

Harrington, D. J., ed. *New Testament Abstracts.* Cambridge, MA: Weston School of Theology, 1956—

Hort, E. *The Bible Book. Resources for Reading the New Testament.* New York: Crossroad, 1983.

Hurd, J. C. *A Bibliography of New Testament Bibliographies.* New York: Seabury, 1966.

Lang, F., ed. *Internationale Zeitschriftenschau für Bibelwissenschaft und Grenzgebiete.* Düsseldorf: Patmos, 1951—

Langevin, P.—E., ed. *Bibliographie Biblique I: 1930-1970; II: 1930-1975.* 2 vols. Quebec: Les Presses de l'Université Laval, 1972, 1978.

*An asterisk before a title indicates that the work is of broad interest and serves as a good introduction to the topic.

Marrow, S. B. *Basic Tools of Biblical Exegesis. A Student's Manual.* Rev. ed. Rome: Biblical Institute Press, 1978.

Martin, R. P. *New Testament Books for Pastor and Teacher.* Philadelphia: Westminster, 1984.

North, R., ed. *Elenchus Bibliographicus Biblicus.* Rome: Biblical Institute Press, 1968—

Wagner, G., ed. *Bibliographical Aids: Exegetical Bibliographies on the Writings of the New Testament.* Rüschlikon, Switzerland: Baptist Theological Seminary, 1973—

_____. *An Exegetical Bibliography of the New Testament. Matthew and Mark.* Macon, GA: Mercer University Press, 1983.

2
Greek Text and Ancient Versions

*Aland, K., et al., eds. *The Greek New Testament*. 3rd rev. ed., corrected. New York—Stuttgart: United Bible Societies, 1983.

Horner, G. W., ed. *The Coptic Version of the New Testament in the Northern Dialect, Otherwise Called Memphitic and Bohairic, with Introduction, Critical Apparatus, and Literal English Translation*. 4 vols. Oxford: Clarendon Press, 1898—1905.

_____. *The Coptic Version of the New Testament in the Southern Dialect, Otherwise Called Sahidic and Thebaic*. 7 vols. Oxford: Clarendon Press, 1911-24.

Jülicher, A., with W. Matzkow and K. Aland, eds. *Itala. Das Neue Testament in altlateinischer Überlieferung*. Berlin: de Gruyter, 1938—

Kilgour, R., ed. *The New Testament in Syriac*. London: British and Foreign Bible Society, 1950.

*Nestle, E., and K. Aland, eds. *Novum Testamentum graece*. 26th ed. New York—Stuttgart: United Bible Societies, 1979.

Ortiz de Urbina, I., ed. *Vetus Evangelium Syrorum et exinde excerptum Diatessaron Tatiani.* Madrid: Consejo Superior de Investigaciones Cientificas, 1967.

Vetus Latina. Die Reste der altlateinischen Bibel nach Petrus Sabatier neu gesammelt und herausgegeben von der Erzabtei Beuron. Freiburg: Herder, 1949—

Weber, R., et al., eds. *Biblia sacra juxta vulgatam versionem.* 2 vols. Stuttgart: Württembergische Bibelanstalt, 1969.

Westcott, B. F. and F. J. A. Hort, eds. *The New Testament in the Original Greek* (1881). 2 vols. Graz: Akademische Druck— und Verlagsanstalt, 1974.

3
Textual Criticism

Aland, K. and B. Aland. *Der Text des Neuen Testaments. Einführung in die wissenschaftlichen Ausgaben sowie in Theorie und Praxis der modernen Textkritik.* Stuttgart: Deutsche Bibelgesellschaft, 1982.

Elliott, J. K. "An Examination of the Twenty-sixth Edition of Nestle-Aland *Novum Testamentum Graece.*" *Journal of Theological Studies* 32 (1981) 19-49.

Epp, E. J. "A Continuing Interlude in New Testament Textual Criticism?" *Harvard Theological Review* 73 (1980) 131-51.

_____ "The Eclectic Method in New Testament Textual Criticism: Solution or Sympton?" *Harvard Theological Review* 69 (1976) 211-57.

_____ *The Theological Tendency of Codex Bezae Cantabrigiensis in Acts.* Cambridge, UK: Cambridge University Press, 1966.

_____ "The Twentieth Century Interlude in New Testament Textual Criticism." *Journal of Biblical Literature* 93 (1974) 386-414.

_____. and G. D. Fee, eds. *New Testament Textual Criticism. Its Significance for Exegesis. Essays in Honor of Bruce M. Metzger.* New York-Oxford: Clarendon Press, 1981.

Fee, G. D. *Papyrus Bodmer II (P66): Its Textual Relationships and Scribal Characteristics.* Salt Lake City, UT: University of Utah Press, 1968.

*Finegan, J. *Encountering New Testament Manuscripts: A Working Introduction to Textual Criticism.* Grand Rapids: Eerdmans, 1974.

Fischer, B. "The Use of Computers in New Testament Studies, with Special Reference to Textual Criticism." *Journal of Theological Studies* 21 (1970) 297-308.

Greenlee, J. H. *Introduction to New Testament Textual Criticism.* Grand Rapids: Eerdmans, 1964.

Kenyon, F. G. *The Text of the Greek Bible.* 3rd ed., rev. by A. W. Adams. London: Duckworth, 1975.

Maas, P. *Textual Criticism.* London—New York: Oxford, 1958.

Martini, C. M. *Il problema della recensionalità del codice B alla luce del papiro Bodmer XIV.* Rome: Biblical Institute Press, 1966.

Metzger, B. M. *Annotated Bibliography of the Textual Criticism of the New Testament, 1914-1939.* Copenhagen: Ejnar Munksgaard, 1955.

_____. *The Early Versions of the New Testament. Their Origin, Transmission, and Limitations.* Oxford: Clarendon Press, 1977.

_____. *Manuscripts of the Greek Bible. An Introduction to Greek Palaeography.* New York-Oxford: Oxford University Press, 1981.

*_____. *A Textual Commentary on the Greek New Testament. A Companion Volume to the United Bible Societies' Greek New Testament (third edition).* London—New York: United Bible Societies, 1971.

_____. *The Text of the New Testament. Its Transmission, Corruption, and Restoration.* 2nd ed. New York—Oxford: Oxford University Press, 1968.

Roberts, C. H. and T. C. Skeat. *The Birth of the Codex.* New York—London: Oxford University Press, 1983.

Suggs, M. J. "The Use of Patristic Evidence in the Search for a Primitive New Testament Text." *New Testament Studies* 4 (1958) 139-47.

Taylor, V. *The Text of the New Testament. A Short Introduction.* New York: St. Martin's Press, 1961.

4
Greek Concordances

*Aland, K., ed. *Vollständige Konkordanz zum griechischen Neuen Testament: Unter Zugrundelegung aller kritischer Textausgaben und des Textus Receptus.* 2 vols. Berlin—New York: de Gruyter, 1975, 1978.

_____, ed. *Computer—Konkordanz zum Novum Testamentum Graece von Nestle-Aland, 26. Auflage und zum Greek New Testament, 3rd edition.* Berlin—New York: de Gruyter, 1980.

Baird, J. A. and D. N. Freedman, eds. *The Computer Bible.* Wooster, OH: Biblical Research Associates, 1971—

*Moulton, W. F., A. S. Geden, and H. K. Moulton. *A Concordance to the Greek Testament according to the Texts of Westcott and Hort, Tischendorf and the English Revisers.* 5th rev. ed. Edinburgh: Clark, 1978.

Morgenthaler, R. *Statistik des neutestamentlichen Wortschatzes.* Zurich—Frankfurt: Gotthelf, 1958.

Neirynck, F. and F. Van Segbroeck. *New Testament Vocabulary. A Companion Volume to the Concordance.* Leuven: Leuven University Press—Peeters, 1984.

Schmoller, A. *Handkonkordanz zum griechischen Neuen Testament.* 9th ed. Stuttgart: Württembergische Bibelanstalt, 1951.

5
Greek Lexica and Grammars

*Bauer, W., F. W. Gingrich, and F. W. Danker. *A Greek—English Lexicon of the New Testament and Other Early Christian Literature.* 2nd ed. Chicago—London: University of Chicago Press, 1979.

Blass, F., A. Debrunner, and F. Rehkopf. *Grammatik des neutestamentlichen Griechisch.* 14th rev. ed. Göttingen: Vandenhoeck & Ruprecht, 1976.

*_____, A. Debrunner, and R. W. Funk. *A Greek Grammar of the New Testament and Other Early Christian Literature.* Chicago: University of Chicago Press, 1961.

Funk, R. W. *A Beginning—Intermediate Grammar of Hellenistic Greek.* 3 vols. Missoula: Scholars, 1977.

Gignac, F. T. *A Grammar of the Greek Papyri of the Roman and Byzantine Periods.* 2 vols. Milan: Istituto Editoriale Cisalpino—La Goliardica, 1976, 1981.

_____. *An Introductory New Testament Greek Course.* Chicago: Loyola University Press, 1973.

Machen, J. G. *New Testament Greek for Beginners.* New York: Macmillan, 1923.

Moule, C. F. D. *An Idiom-Book of New Testament Greek.* 2nd ed. Cambridge, UK: Cambridge University Press, 1959.

Moulton, J. H., F. W. Howard, and N. Turner. *A Grammar of New Testament Greek.* 4 vols. Edinburgh: Clark, 1929, 1949, 1963, 1976.

_____ and G. Milligan. *The Vocabulary of the Greek Testament Illustrated from the Papyri and Other Non-Literary Sources.* 2nd ed. London: Hodder and Stoughton, 1957.

Rienecker, F. *A Linguistic Key to the Greek New Testament.* 2 vols. Edited by C. L. Rogers. Grand Rapids: Zondervan, 1976, 1980.

Whittaker, M. *New Testament Greek Grammar. An Introduction.* Rev. ed. London: SCM, 1980.

*Zerwick, M. and M. Grosvenor. *A Grammatical Analysis of the Greek New Testament.* 2 vols. Rome: Biblical Institute Press, 1974, 1979.

6
Modern English Translations

Good News Bible with Deuterocanonicals/Apocrypha. The Bible in Today's English Version. New York: American Bible Society, 1979.

The Holy Bible. New International Version. Containing The Old Testament and The New Testament. Grand Rapids: Zondervan, 1978.

The Holy Bible Containing the Old and New Testaments. Revised Standard Version. New York: United Bible Societies, 1971.

The Jerusalem Bible. Garden City, NY: Doubleday, 1966.

The New American Bible. Translated from the Original Languages with Critical Use of All the Ancient Sources. Paterson, NJ: St. Anthony Guild, 1970.

The New English Bible with the Apocrypha. New York: Oxford University Press and Cambridge University Press, 1970.

7
English Concordances

Bailey, L. R. "What a Concordance Can do for You. The Bible Word by Word." *Biblical Archaeology Review* 10 (1984) 60-67.

Darton, M., ed. *Modern Concordance to the New Testament.* Garden City, NY: Doubleday, 1976.

Elder, E., ed. *Concordance to the New English Bible: New Testament.* Grand Rapids: Zondervan, 1964.

Goodrick, E. W. and J. R. Kohlenberger, eds. *The NIV Complete Concordance. The Complete English Concordance to the New International Version.* Grand Rapids: Zondervan, 1981.

Hartdegen, S. J., ed. *Nelson's Complete Concordance of the New American Bible.* Collegeville, MN: Liturgical Press, 1977; Nashville: Nelson.

*Morrison, C., ed. *An Analytical Concordance to the Revised Standard Version of the New Testament.* Philadelphia: Westminster, 1979.

Robinson, D., ed. *Concordance to the Good News Bible.* Swindon, UK: Bible Society, 1983.

Strong, J. *The New Strong's Exhaustive Concordance of the Bible.* Nashville: Nelson, 1984.

8
Guides to English Translations

*Bailey, L. R., ed. *The Word of God. A Guide to English Versions of the Bible.* Atlanta: John Knox, 1982.

Beekman, J. and J. Callow. *Translating the Word of God.* Grand Rapids: Zondervan, 1974.

Bruce, F. F. *History of the Bible in English. From the earliest versions.* 3rd ed. New York: Oxford University Press, 1978.

Kubo, S. and W. F. Specht. *So Many Versions? Twentieth-Century English Versions of the Bible.* Rev. ed. Grand Rapids: Zondervan, 1983.

Lewis, J. P. *The English Bible from KJV to NIV. A History and Evaluation.* Grand Rapids: Baker, 1981.

Mays, J. L., ed. *Interpretation* 32 (1978) 115-70.

McCall, D., ed. *Review and Expositor* 76 (1979) 297-416.

Nida, E. A. and C. R. Taber. *The Theory and Practice of Translation.* Leiden: Brill, 1969.

9
Biblical Linguistics

Barr, J. *Biblical Words for Time.* Naperville, IL: Allenson, 1962; London: SCM.

*_____. *The Semantics of Biblical Language.* New York: Oxford University Press, 1961.

Black, M. *An Aramaic Approach to the Gospels and Acts.* 3rd rev. ed. New York—London: Oxford University Press, 1968.

Brock, S. P., C. T. Fritsch, and S. Jellicoe, eds. *A Classified Bibliography of the Septuagint.* Leiden: Brill, 1973.

Caird, G. B. *The Language and Imagery of the Bible.* Philadelphia: Westminster, 1980.

Fitzmyer, J. A. "The Aramaic Language and the Study of the New Testament." *Journal of Biblical Literature* 99 (1980) 5-21.

_____. "The Contribution of Qumran Aramaic to the Study of the New Testament." *New Testament Studies* 20 (1974) 382-407.

_____. "The Languages of Palestine in the First Century A.D." *Catholic Biblical Quarterly* 32 (1970) 501-31.

_____. *A Wandering Aramean. Collected Aramaic Essays.* Missoula: Scholars, 1979.

_____ and D. J. Harrington. *A Manual of Palestinian Aramaic Texts (Second Century B.C.—Second Century A.D.).* Rome: Biblical Institute Press, 1978.

Hill, D. *Greek Words and Hebrew Meanings: Studies in the Semantics of Soteriological Terms.* New York— London: Cambridge University Press, 1968.

Louw, J. P. *Semantics of New Testament Greek.* Philadelphia: Fortress, 1982; Chico: Scholars.

Mussies, G. "Greek as the Vehicle of Early Christianity." *New Testament Studies* 29 (1983) 356-69.

_____. "The Use of Hebrew and Aramaic in the Greek New Testament." *New Testament Studies* 30 (1984) 416-32.

*Sevenster, J. N. *Do You Know Greek? How Much Greek Could the First Christians Have Known?* Leiden: Brill, 1968.

Spicq, C. *Notes de Lexicographique néo-testamentaire.* 2 vols., supplement. Fribourg: Editions Universitaires, 1978, 1982; Göttingen: Vandenhoeck & Ruprecht.

Turner, N. *Christian Words.* Edinburgh: Clark, 1980.

10
Biblical Dictionaries
and
Encyclopedias

Balz, H. and G. Schneider, eds. *Exegetisches Wörterbuch zum Neuen Testament.* Stuttgart—Berlin—Cologne—Mainz: Kohlhammer, 1978—

Bauer, J. B., ed. *Encyclopedia of Biblical Theology: The Complete Sacramentum Verbi.* New York: Crossroad, 1981.

Blair, E. P., ed. *Abingdon Bible Handbook.* Nashville: Abingdon, 1975.

Bromiley, G. W., ed. *The International Standard Bible Encyclopedia.* 4 vols. Grand Rapids: Eerdmans, 1979—

Brown, C., ed. *The New International Dictionary of New Testament Theology.* 3 vols. Grand Rapids: Zondervan, 1975.

*Buttrick, G. A., et al., eds. *The Interpreter's Dictionary of the Bible. An Illustrated Encyclopedia.* 5 vols. New York—Nashville: Abingdon, 1962, 1976.

Cazelles, H. and A. Feuillet, eds. *Supplément au Diction-naire de la Bible*. Paris: Letouzey et Ané, 1928—

Gehman, H. S., ed. *The New Westminster Dictionary of the Bible* (1970). Philadelphia: Westminster, 1982.

Hartman, L. F., ed. *Encyclopedic Dictionary of the Bible*. New York—London: McGraw-Hill, 1963.

Hillyer, N. et al., eds. *The Illustrated Bible Dictionary*. 3 vols. Leicester, UK: Inter-Varsity, 1980; Wheaton, IL: Tyndale.

*Kittel, G. and G. Friedrich, eds. *Theological Dictionary of the New Testament*. 10 vols. Edited and translated by G. W. Bromiley. Grand Rapids: Eerdmans, 1964-76.

Léon-Dufour, X., ed. *Dictionary of Biblical Theology*. New York—Tournai: Desclée, 1967.

_____. *Dictionary of the New Testament*. San Francisco: Harper & Row, 1980; Toronto: Fitzhenry & Whiteside.

McKenzie, J. L. *Dictionary of the Bible*. Milwaukee, WI: Bruce, 1965.

Miller, M. S. and J. L. Miller, eds. *Harper's Dictionary of the Bible*. Rev. ed. San Francisco: Harper & Row, 1978.

11
New Testament Introductions

Bornkamm, G. *The New Testament. A Guide to Its Writings.* Philadelphia: Fortress, 1973.

Childs, B. S. *The New Testament as Canon: An Introduction.* Philadelphia: Fortress, 1985.

Cullmann, O. *The New Testament. An Introduction for the General Reader.* Philadelphia: Westminster, 1968.

Fuller, R. H. *A Critical Introduction to the New Testament.* London: Gerald Duckworth, 1966.

George, A. and P. Grelot, eds. *Introduction à la Bible. Tome III: Introduction critique au Nouveau Testament.* 5 vols. Tournai—Paris: Desclée, 1976-77.

Guthrie, D. *New Testament Introduction.* Rev. ed. Downers Grove, IL: Inter-Varsity, 1971.

Kee, H. C. *Understanding the New Testament.* 4th ed. Englewood Cliffs, NJ: Prentice-Hall, 1983.

Klijn, A. F. J. *An Introduction to the New Testament.* Rev. ed. Leiden: Brill, 1980.

Koester, H. *Introduction to the New Testament.* 2 vols. Philadelphia: Fortress, 1982.

*Kümmel, W. G. *Introduction to the New Testament.* Nashville: Abingdon, 1975.

Lohse, E. *The Formation of the New Testament.* Nashville: Abingdon, 1981.

Martin, R. P. *New Testament Foundations: A Guide for Christian Students.* 2 vols. Grand Rapids: Eerdmans, 1975, 1978.

Marxsen, W. *Introduction to the New Testament. An Approach to its Problems.* Philadelphia: Fortress, 1968.

Moule, C. F. D. *The Birth of the New Testament.* 3rd ed. San Francisco: Harper & Row, 1981; Toronto: Fitzhenry & Whiteside.

Perkins, P. *Reading the New Testament. An Introduction.* New York—Ramsey, NJ: Paulist, 1978.

Perrin, N. and D. C. Duling. *The New Testament: An Introduction. Proclamation and Parenesis, Myth and History.* 2nd ed. New York: Harcourt Brace Jovanovich, 1982.

Robinson, J. A. T. *Redating the New Testament.* Philadelphia: Westminster, 1976.

Spivey, R. A. and D. M. Smith. *Anatomy of the New Testament. A Guide to Its Structure and Meaning.* 3rd ed. New York: Macmillan, 1982; London: Collier Macmillan.

Tyson, J. B. *The New Testament and Early Christianity.* New York: Macmillan, 1984; London: Collier Macmillan.

Wikenhauser, A. and J. Schmid. *Einleitung in das New Testament.* 6th rev. ed. Freiburg—Vienna: Herder, 1973.

12
One-Volume Commentaries

Black, M. and H. H. Rowley, eds. *Peake's Commentary on the Bible.* New York—London: Nelson, 1962.

*Brown, R. E., J. A. Fitzmyer, and R. A. Murphy, eds. *The Jerome Biblical Commentary.* 2 vols. Englewood Cliffs, NJ: Prentice-Hall, 1968.

Fuller, R. C., L. Johnston, and C. Kearns, eds. *A New Catholic Commentary on Holy Scripture.* Camden, NJ— London: Nelson, 1969.

Laymon, C. M., ed. *The Interpreter's One-Volume Commentary on the Bible.* Nashville—New York: Abingdon, 1971.

II. Interpretation

13
Exegetical Methodology

*Collins, R. F. *Introduction to the New Testament.* Garden City, NY: Doubleday, 1983.

Conzelmann, H. and A. Lindemann. *Arbeitsbuch zum Neuen Testament.* 5th rev. ed. Tübingen: Mohr-Siebeck, 1980.

Doty, W. G. *Contemporary New Testament Interpretation.* Englewood Cliffs, NJ: Prentice-Hall, 1972.

Fee, G. D. *New Testament Exegesis. A Handbook for Students and Pastors.* Philadelphia: Westminster, 1983.

Güttgemanns, E. *Candid Questions Concerning Gospel Form Criticism. A Methodological Sketch of the Fundamental Problematics of Form and Redaction Criticism.* Pittsburgh: Pickwick, 1979.

Haacker, K. *Neutestamentliche Wissenschaft. Eine Einführung in Fragestellungen und Methoden.* Wuppertal: Brockhaus, 1981.

*Harrington, D. J. *Interpreting the New Testament. A Practical Guide.* Wilmington: Michael Glazier, 1979.

Hayes, J. H. and C. R. Holladay. *Biblical Exegesis. A Beginner's Handbook*. Atlanta: John Knox, 1982.

Kaiser, O. and W. G. Kümmel. *Exegetical Method. A Student's Handbook*. Rev. ed. New York: Seabury, 1981.

Koch, K. *The Growth of the Biblical Tradition. The Form-Critical Method*. New York: Scribner's, 1971.

Lohfink, G. *The Bible: Now I Get It. A Form-Criticism Handbook*. Garden City, NY: Doubleday, 1979.

Marshall, I. H., ed. *New Testament Interpretation. Essays on Principles and Methods*. Grand Rapids: Eerdmans, 1977; Exeter, UK: Paternoster.

McKnight, E. V. *What is Form Criticism?* Philadelphia: Fortress, 1969.

Palmer, H. *The Logic of Gospel Criticism. An Account of the methods and arguments used by textual, documentary, source and form critics of the New Testament*. New York: St. Martin's, 1968; London-Toronto: Macmillan.

Perrin, N. *What is Redaction Criticism?* Philadelphia: Fortress, 1969.

Sandmel, S. "Parallelomania." *Journal of Biblical Literature* 81 (1962) 1-13.

Schreiner, J., ed. *Einführung in den Methoden der biblischen Exegese*. Würzburg: Echter, 1971.

Soulen, R. N. *Handbook of Biblical Criticism*. 2nd rev. ed. Atlanta: John Knox, 1981.

Strecker, G. and U. Schnelle. *Einführung in die neutesta-mentliche Exegese.* Göttingen: Vandenhoeck & Ruprecht, 1983.

Turner, N. *Handbook for Biblical Studies.* Philadelphia: Westminster, 1982.

Wadsworth, M., ed. *Ways of Reading the Bible.* Brighton, UK: Harvester Press, 1981; Totowa, NJ: Barnes & Noble Books.

Zimmermann, H. *Neutestamentliche Methodenlehre. Darstellung der historisch-kritischen Methode.* 6th rev. ed. Stuttgart: Katholisches Bibelwerk, 1978.

14
Literary Approaches

Alonso Schökel, L. *The Inspired Word. Scripture in the Light of Language and Literature.* New York: Herder & Herder, 1965.

Barr, J. "Reading the Bible as Literature." *Bulletin of the John Rylands University Library of Manchester* 56 (1973) 10-33.

Beardslee, W. A. *Literary Criticism of the New Testament.* Philadelphia: Fortress, 1970.

Frye, N. *The Great Code. The Bible and Literature.* New York—London: Harcourt Brace Jovanovich, 1982.

Gottcent, J. H. *The Bible as Literature. A Selective Bibliography.* Boston: Hall, 1979.

Henn, T. R. *The Bible as Literature.* New York: Oxford University Press, 1970.

*Kennedy, G. A. *New Testament Interpretation through Rhetorical Criticism.* Chapel Hill, NC—London: University of North Carolina Press, 1984.

Petersen, N. R. *Literary Criticism for New Testament Critics.* Philadelphia: Fortress, 1978.

Ryken, L., ed. *The New Testament in Literary Criticism.* New York: Frederick Ungar Publishing, 1984.

Via, D. O. *Kerygma and Comedy in the New Testament. A Structuralist Approach to Hermeneutic.* Philadelphia: Fortress, 1975.

*Wilder, A. N. *The Language of the Gospel. Early Christian Rhetoric.* New York—Evanston, IL: Harper & Row, 1964.

_____. *The New Voice. Religion, Literature, and Hermeneutics.* New York: Herder & Herder, 1969.

_____. *Theopoetic. Theology and the Religious Imagination.* Philadelphia: Fortress, 1976.

15
Social-Science Approaches

Best, T. F. "The Sociological Study of the New Testament: Promise and Peril of a New Discipline." *Scottish Journal of Theology* 36 (1983) 181-94.

*Gager, J. G. *Kingdom and Community. The Social World of Early Christianity.* Englewood Cliffs, NJ: Prentice-Hall, 1975.

_____. "Shall We Marry Our Enemies? Sociology and the New Testament." *Interpretation* 36 (1982) 256-65.

Gottwald, N. K., ed. *The Bible and Liberation. Political and Social Hermeneutics.* Rev. ed. Maryknoll, NY: Orbis Books, 1983.

Johnson, A. M., ed. *Structuralism and Biblical Hermeneutics. A Collection of Essays.* Pittsburgh: Pickwick, 1979.

Kee, H. C. *Christian Origins in Sociological Perspective. Methods and Resources.* Philadelphia: Westminster, 1980.

Malina, B. *The New Testament World. Insights from Cultural Anthropology.* Atlanta: John Knox, 1981.

_____. "The Social Sciences and Biblical Interpretation." *Interpretation* 36 (1982) 229-42.

Miranda, J. P. *Marx and the Bible.* Maryknoll, NY: Orbis, 1974.

Patte, D. *What is Structural Exegesis?* Philadelphia: Fortress, 1976.

_____ and A. Patte. *Structural Exegesis: From Theory to Practice. Exegesis of Mark 15 and 16. Hermeneutical Implications.* Philadelphia: Fortress, 1978.

Rollins, W. *Jung and the Bible.* Atlanta: John Knox, 1983.

Scroggs, R. "The Sociological Interpretation of the New Testament: The Present State of Research." *New Testament Studies* 26 (1980) 164-79.

*Theissen, G. *Sociology of Early Palestinian Christianity.* Philadelphia: Fortress, 1978.

Wink, W. *The Bible in Human Transformation. Toward a New Paradigm for Biblical Study.* Philadelphia: Fortress, 1973.

_____. *Transforming Bible Study. A Leader's Guide.* Nashville: Abingdon, 1980.

16
Hermeneutics

Achtemeier, P. J. *An Introduction to the New Hermeneutic.* Philadelphia: Westminster, 1969.

Barr, J. *Fundamentalism.* Philadelphia: Westminster, 1978.

_____. *The Bible in the Modern World.* New York: Harper & Row, 1973.

*Brown, R. E. *The Critical Meaning of the Bible.* New York—Ramsey, NJ: Paulist, 1981.

Bultmann, R. *Jesus Christ and Mythology.* New York: Charles Scribner's Sons, 1958.

_____. *New Testament and Mythology and Other Basic Writings.* Philadelphia: Fortress, 1984.

Funk, R. W. *Language, Hermeneutic, and Word of God. The Problem of Language in the New Testament and Contemporary Theology.* New York—Evanston, IL—London: Harper & Row, 1966.

Greenspahn, F. E., ed. *Scripture in the Jewish and Christian Traditions: Authority, Interpretation, Relevance.* Nashville: Abingdon, 1982.

*Hagen, K. et al. *The Bible in the Churches. How Different Christians Interpret the Scriptures.* New York— Mahwah, NJ: Paulist, 1985.

Kelsey, D. H. *The Uses of Scripture in Recent Theology.* Philadelphia: Fortress, 1975.

Levie, J. *The Bible, Word of God in Words of Men.* New York: P. J. Kenedy, 1962.

McKnight, E. V. *Meaning in Texts. The Historical Shaping of a Narrative Hermeneutics.* Philadelphia: Fortress, 1978.

*Megivern, J. J., ed. *Bible Interpretation. Official Catholic Teachings.* Wilmington, NC: Consortium Books/ McGrath Publishing, 1978.

Nineham, D. *The Use and Abuse of the Bible. A Study of the Bible in an Age of Rapid Cultural Change.* New York: Barnes & Noble/Harper & Row, 1977.

Ricoeur, P. "Biblical Hermeneutics." *Semeia* 4 (1975) 27-148.

——————— *Essays on Biblical Interpretation.* Philadelphia: Fortress, 1980.

Schüssler Fiorenza, E. *Bread Not Stone. The Challenge of Feminist Biblical Interpretation.* Boston: Beacon Press, 1984.

Smart, J. D. *The Interpretation of Scripture.* Philadelphia: Westminster, 1961.

_____. *The Strange Silence of the Bible in the Church.* Philadelphia: Westminster, 1970.

Soares-Prabhu, G. M. "Toward An Indian Interpretation of the Bible." *Biblebhashyam* 6 (1980) 151-70.

Stendhal, K. *Meanings. The Bible as Document and Guide.* Philadelphia: Fortress, 1984.

*Thistelton, A. C. *The Two Horizons. New Testament Hermeneutics and Philosophical Description with Special Reference to Heidegger, Bultmann, Gadamer, and Wittgenstein.* Grand Rapids: Eerdmans, 1980.

17
History of Interpretation

Ackroyd, P. R. et al., eds. *The Cambridge History of the Bible*. 3 vols. Cambridge, UK—New York: Cambridge University Press, 1963, 1969, 1970.

*Grant, R. M. and D. Tracy. *A Short History of the Interpretation of the Bible*. 2nd rev. ed. Philadelphia: Fortress, 1984.

Henry, P. *New Directions in New Testament Study*. Philadelphia: Westminster, 1979.

Kümmel, W. G. *The New Testament: The History of the Investigation of Its Problems*. Nashville—New York: Abingdon, 1972.

*Neill, S. *The Interpretation of the New Testament 1861-1961. The Firth Lectures*. New York—London: Oxford University Press, 1964.

18
Canon

Aland, K. "The Problem of Anonymity and Pseudonymity in Christian Literature of the First Two Centuries." *Journal of Theological Studies* 12 (1961) 39-49.

_____ *The Problem of the New Testament Canon.* London: Mowbray, 1962.

Appel, N. *Kanon und Kirche. Die Kanonkrise im heutigen Protestantismus als kontroverstheologisches Problem.* Paderborn: Bonifacius-Druckerei, 1964.

_____ "The New Testament Canon: Historical Process and Spirit's Witness." *Theological Studies* 32 (1971) 627-46.

Barr, J. *Holy Scripture. Canon, Authority, Criticism.* Philadelphia: Westminster, 1983.

Best, E. "Scripture, Tradition, and the Canon of the New Testament." *Bulletin of the John Rylands University Library of Manchester* 61 (1979) 258-89.

Dunn, J. D. G. "Levels of Canonical Authority." *Horizons in Biblical Theology* 4 (1982) 13-60.

Farmer, W. R. *Jesus and the Gospel. Tradition, Scripture, and Canon.* Philadelphia: Fortress, 1982.

_____ and D. M. Farkasfalvy. *The Formation of the New Testament Canon. An Ecumenical Approach.* New York—Ramsey, NJ—Toronto: Paulist, 1983.

Käsemann, E., ed. *Das Neue Testament als Kanon. Dokumentation und kritische Analyse zur gegenwärtigen Diskussion.* Göttingen: Vandenhoeck & Ruprecht, 1970.

Metzger, B. M. "Literary Forgeries and Canonical Pseudepigrapha." *Journal of Biblical Literature* 91 (1972) 3-24.

Murray, R. "How Did the Church Determine the Canon of Scripture?" *Heythrop Journal* 11 (1970) 115-26.

*von Campenhausen, H. *The Formation of the Christian Bible.* Philadelphia: Fortress, 1972.

19
Biblical Inspiration

Abraham, W. J. *The Divine Inspiration of Holy Scripture.* Oxford—New York: Oxford University Press, 1981.

_____. *Divine Revelation and the Limits of Historical Criticism.* New York: Oxford University Press, 1982.

Achtemeier, P. J. *The Inspiration of Scripture. Problems and Proposals.* Philadelphia: Westminster, 1980.

Benoit, P. *Aspects of Biblical Inspiration.* Chicago: Priory Press, 1965.

Burtchaell, J. T. *Catholic Theories of Biblical Inspiration since 1810. A Review and Critique.* New York: Cambridge University Press, 1969.

Marshall, I. *Biblical Inspiration.* Grand Rapids: Eerdmans, 1983.

McKenzie, J. L. "The Social Character of Inspiration." *Catholic Biblical Quarterly* 24 (1962) 115-24.

Rahner, K. *Inspiration in the Bible.* New York: Herder & Herder, 1961.

*Vawter, B. *Biblical Inspiration.* Philadelphia: Westminster, 1972; London: Hutchinson.

20
Sensus Plenior

Brown, R. E. *The Sensus Plenior of Sacred Scripture.* Baltimore, MD: St. Mary's University, 1955.

_____ "The *Sensus Plenior* in the Last Ten Years." *Catholic Biblical Quarterly* 25 (1963) 262-85.

*_____ "The Problems of the *Sensus Plenior*." *Ephemerides Theologicae Lovanienses* 43 (1967) 460-69.

Robinson, J. M. "Scripture and Theological Method. A Protestant Study in *Sensus Plenior*." *Catholic Biblical Quarterly* 27 (1965) 6-27.

Vawter, B. "The Fuller Sense: Some Considerations." *Catholic Biblical Quarterly* 26 (1964) 85-96.

21
Biblical Authority

Bartlett, D. L. *The Shape of Scriptural Authority.* Philadelphia: Fortress, 1983.

Bratcher, R. G. "Toward Definition of the Authority of the Bible." *Perspectives in Religious Studies* 6 (1979) 109-20.

*Dunn, J. D. G. "The Authority of Scripture According to Scripture." *Churchman* 96 (1982) 104-22, 201-25.

Flessemann-van Leer, E., ed. *The Bible. Its Authority and Interpretation in the Ecumenical Movement.* Geneva: World Council of Churches, 1980.

Reventlow, H. G. *The Authority of the Bible and the Rise of the Modern World.* Philadelphia: Fortress, 1985.

Rogers, J. B. and D. K. McKim. *The Authority and Interpretation of the Bible. An Historical Approach.* New York—Hagerstown—San Francisco—London: Harper & Row, 1979; Toronto: Fitzhenry & Whiteside.

Woodbridge, J. D. *Biblical Authority. A Critique of the Rogers/McKim Proposal.* Grand Rapids: Zondervan, 1982.

22
The Bible in Church Life Today

Best, E. *From Text to Sermon. Responsible Use of the New Testament in Preaching.* Atlanta: John Knox, 1978.

Burke, J., ed. *A New Look at Preaching.* Wilmington: Michael Glazier, 1983.

*Fuller, R. H. *The Use of the Bible in Preaching.* Philadelphia: Fortress, 1981.

LaVerdiere, E. *The New Testament in the Life of the Church. Evangelization, Prayer, Catechetics, Homiletics.* Notre Dame, IN: Ave Maria Press, 1980.

Vogels, W. "Biblical Exegesis and the Homily: Two Decades in retrospect and prospect." *Science et Esprit* 34 (1982) 289-314.

——————— *Reading & Preaching the Bible.* Wilmington: Michael Glazier, 1985.

III. Gospels and Acts

23
Gospel Synopses

Aland, K., ed. *Synopsis Quattuor Evangeliorum: Locis parallelis evangeliorum apocryphorum et patrum adhibitis.* 9th ed. Stuttgart: Deutsche Bibelstiftung, 1976.

_____ *Synopsis of the Four Gospels. English Edition.* New York: United Bible Societies, 1982.

*_____ *Synopsis of the Four Gospels. Greek-English Edition of the Synopsis Quattuor Evangeliorum.* Stuttgart—New York: United Bible Societies, 1976.

Huck, A. and H. Greeven, eds. *Synopse der drei ersten Evangelien mit Beigabe der johanneischen Parallelstellen. Synopsis of the First Three Gospels with the Addition of the Johannine Parallels.* 13th rev. ed. Tübingen: Mohr-Siebeck, 1981.

Orchard, J. B., ed. *A Synopsis of the Four Gospels in Greek Arranged according to the Two-Gospel Hypothesis.* Macon, GA: Mercer University Press, 1983; Edinburgh: Clark.

_____. *A Synopsis of the Four Gospels in a New Translation Arranged according to the Two-Gospel Hypothesis.* Macon, GA: Mercer University Press, 1982.

Swanson, R. J., ed. *The Horizontal Line Synopsis of the Gospels (Revised).* Pasadena, GA: William Carey Library, 1984.

*Throckmorton, B. H., ed. *Gospel Parallels. A Synopsis of the First Three Gospels.* 4th rev. ed. Nashville—New York: Nelson, 1979.

24
Sayings Source Q

Delobel, J., ed. *Logia. Les Paroles de Jésus—The Sayings of Jesus.* Leuven: Peeters—Leuven University Press, 1982.

Edwards, R. A. *A Concordance to Q.* Missoula: Society of Biblical Literature and Scholars Press, 1975.

*_____. *A Theology of Q. Eschatology, Prophecy, and Wisdom.* Philadelphia: Fortress, 1975.

Lührmann, D. *Die Redaktion der Logienquelle.* Neukirchen-Vluyn: Neukirchener, 1969.

Polag, A. *Die Christologie der Logienquelle.* Neukirchen-Vluyn: Neukirchener, 1977.

_____. *Fragmenta Q. Textheft zur Logienquelle.* Neukirchen-Vluyn: Neukirchener, 1979.

Schenk, W. *Synopse zur Redenquelle der Evangelien. Q-Synopse und Rekonstruktion in deutscher Übersetzung mit kurzen Erläuterungen.* Düsseldorf: Patmos, 1981.

Zeller, D. *Kommentar zum Logienquelle.* Stuttgart: Katholisches Bibelwerk, 1984.

25
Synoptic Tradition

Beare, F. W. *The Earliest Records of Jesus.* New York—Nashville: Abingdon, 1962.

Benoit, P. and M.—E. Boismard. *Synopse des quatres Evangiles en français, Tome II: Commentaire.* Paris: Cerf, 1972.

*Bultmann, R. *The History of the Synoptic Tradition.* 2nd ed. Oxford: Blackwell, 1968.

de Solages, B. *La composition des évangiles de Luc et de Matthieu et leurs sources.* Leiden: Brill, 1973.

*Dibelius, M. *From Tradition to Gospel.* 2nd rev. ed. New York: Scribner's, 1965.

Dungan, D. L. *The Sayings of Jesus in the Churches of Paul. The Use of the Synoptic Tradition in the Regulation of Early Church Life.* Philadelphia: Fortress, 1971.

_____ "Theory of Synopsis Construction." *Biblica* 61 (1980) 305-29.

Farmer, W. R. *The Synoptic Problem. A Critical Analysis.* Rev. ed. Dillsboro, NC: Western North Carolina Press, 1976.

Fitzmyer, J. A. "The Priority of Mark and the 'Q' Source in Luke." *Perspective* 11 (1970) 131-70.

Gaboury, A. *La structure des évangiles synoptiques. La structure-type à l'origine des synoptiques.* Leiden: Brill, 1970.

Gerhardsson, B. *Memory and Manuscript. Oral Tradition and Written Transmission in Rabbinic Judaism and Early Christianity.* Lund: C.W.K. Gleerup, 1961.

_____ *The Origins of the Gospel Traditions.* Philadelphia: Fortress, 1979.

Hawkins, J. C. *Horae Synopticae. Contributions to the Study of the Synoptic Problem* (1899; 2nd ed., 1909). Grand Rapids: Baker, 1968.

*Kümmel, W. G. *Introduction to the New Testament.* Nashville—New York: Abingdon, 1975. Pp. 38-80.

Longstaff, T. R. W. *Evidence of Conflation in Mark? A Study in the Synoptic Problem.* Missoula: Scholars, 1977.

Neirynck, F. *The Minor Agreements of Matthew and Luke against Mark with a Cumulative List.* Gembloux: Duculot, 1974.

Orchard, J. B. *Matthew, Luke & Mark.* Manchester, UK: Koinonia Press, 1976.

_____ and T. R. W. Longstaff, eds. *J. J. Griesbach: Synoptic and text-critical studies 1776-1976.* New York—London: Cambridge University Press, 1978.

Rist, J. M. *On the Independence of Matthew and Mark.* Cambridge—London—New York—Melbourne: Cambridge University Press, 1978.

Rolland, P. *Les Premiers évangiles. Un nouveau regard sur le problème synoptique.* Paris: Cerf, 1984.

Sanders, E. P. *The Tendencies of the Synoptic Tradition.* New York: Cambridge University Press, 1969.

Stoldt, H.—H. *History and Criticism of the Marcan Hypothesis.* Macon, GA: Mercer University Press, 1980; Edinburgh: Clark.

Tuckett, C. M. *The Revival of the Griesbach Hypothesis. An Analysis and Appraisal.* Cambridge, UK—London—New York: Cambridge University Press, 1983.

_____, ed. *Synoptic Studies: The Ampleforth Conference of 1982 and 1983.* Sheffield, UK: JSOT Press, 1984.

Tyson, J. B. and T. R. W. Longstaff. *Synoptic Abstract.* Wooster, OH: Biblical Research Associates, 1978.

Walker, W. O., ed. *The Relationships among the Gospels. An Interdisciplinary Dialogue.* San Antonio, TX: Trinity University Press, 1978.

26
Matthew: Commentaries

Beare, F. W. *The Gospel According to Matthew. Translation, Introduction and Commentary.* San Francisco: Harper & Row, 1981.

Bonnard, P. *L'Evangile selon Saint Matthieu.* 2nd rev. ed. Neuchâtel: Delachaux & Niestlé, 1970.

Fenton, J. C. *St. Matthew.* Philadelphia: Westminster, 1978.

Gundry, R. H. *Matthew: A Commentary on His Literary and Theological Art.* Grand Rapids: Eerdmans, 1982.

Hill, D. *The Gospel of Matthew.* London: Oliphants, 1972.

McNeile, A. H. *The Gospel According to St. Matthew. The Greek Text with Introduction and Notes* (1915). Grand Rapids: Baker, 1980.

*Meier, J. P. *Matthew.* Wilmington: Michael Glazier, 1980.

Sabourin, L. *The Gospel According to St. Matthew.* 2 vols. Bombay: St. Paul Publications, 1982.

*Schweizer, E. *The Good News According to Matthew.* Atlanta: John Knox, 1975.

27
Matthew: Studies

*Bornkamm, G., G. Barth, and H. J. Held. *Tradition and Interpretation in Matthew*. 2nd rev. ed. London: SCM, 1982.

Cope, O. L. *Matthew: A Scribe Trained for the Kingdom of Heaven*. Washington: Catholic Biblical Association, 1976.

Davies, W. D. *The Setting of the Sermon on the Mount*. New York—London: Cambridge University Press, 1964.

Didier, M., ed. *L'Evangile selon Matthieu. Redaction et théologie*. Gembloux: Duculot, 1972.

Goulder, M. D. *Midrash and Lection in Matthew*. London: S.P.C.K., 1974.

Guelich, R. A. *The Sermon on the Mount. A Foundation for Understanding*. Waco, TX: Word Books, 1982.

Hare, D. R. A. *The Theme of Jewish Persecution of Christians in the Gospel According to St. Matthew*. New York—London: Cambridge University Press, 1967.

Kingsbury, J. D. *Matthew: Structure, Christology, Kingdom.* Philadelphia: Fortress, 1975.

Lange, J., ed. *Das Matthäus—Evangelium.* Darmstadt: Wissenschaftliche Buchgesellschaft, 1980.

Meier, J. P. *Law and History in Matthew's Gospel. A Redactional Study of Mt. 5:17-48.* Rome: Biblical Institute Press, 1976.

_____ *The Vision of Matthew: Christ, Church and Morality in the First Gospel.* New York: Paulist, 1979.

Przybylski, B. *Righteousness in Matthew and His World of Thought.* New York—Cambridge, UK—London: Cambridge University Press, 1980.

*Senior, D. *What Are They Saying About Matthew?* New York—Ramsey, NJ: Paulist, 1983.

Shuler, P. L. *A Genre for the Gospels. The Biographical Character of Matthew.* Philadelphia: Fortress, 1982.

Stanton, G. "The Origin and Purpose of Matthew's Gospel: Matthean Scholarship from 1945 to 1980." *Aufstieg und Niedergang der römischen Welt.* 25/3, ed. W. Haase. Berlin—New York: de Gruyter, 1985. Pp. 1889-1951.

_____, ed. *The Interpretation of Matthew.* Philadelphia: Fortress, 1983; London: S.P.C.K.

Stendahl, K. *The School of St. Matthew and its Use of the Old Testament.* 2nd ed. Philadelphia: Fortress, 1968.

Strecker, G. *Der Weg der Gerechtigkeit. Untersuchung zur Theologie des Matthäus.* Göttingen: Vandenhoeck & Ruprecht, 1962.

Suggs, M. J. *Wisdom, Christology, and Law in Matthew's Gospel.* Cambridge, MA: Harvard University Press, 1970.

Thompson, W. G. *Matthew's Advice to a Divided Community. Mt. 17, 22-18, 35.* Rome: Biblical Institute Press, 1970.

Thysman, R. *Communauté et directives ethiques: La Catechese de Matthieu.* Gembloux: Duculot, 1974.

Trilling, W. *Das wahre Israel. Studien zur Theologie des Matthäusevangeliums.* 3rd ed. Munich: Kösel, 1964.

Walker, R. *Die Heilsgeschichte im ersten Evangelium.* Göttingen: Vandenhoeck & Ruprecht, 1967.

Zumstein, J. *La condition du croyant dans l'évangile selon Matthieu.* Fribourg: Etudes Universitaires, 1977; Göttingen: Vandenhoeck & Ruprecht.

28
Mark: Commentaries

Anderson, H. *The Gospel of Mark* (1976). Grand Rapids: Eerdmans, 1981; London: Marshall, Morgan & Scott.

Cranfield, C. E. *The Gospel According to St. Mark: An Introduction and Commentary.* 2nd rev. ed. (1963). Cambridge, UK: Cambridge University Press, 1979.

Ernst, J. *Das Evangelium nach Markus. Übersetzt und erklärt.* Regensburg: F. Pustet, 1981.

Gnilka, J. *Das Evangelium nach Markus.* 2 vols. Zurich—Einsiedeln—Cologne: Benziger, 1978; Neukirchen—Vluyn: Neukirchener.

*Harrington, W. *Mark.* Wilmington: Michael Glazier, 1979.

Hurtado, L. W. *Mark.* San Francisco: Harper & Row, 1983.

Lane, W. *Mark.* Grand Rapids: Eerdmans, 1973.

*Nineham, D. E. *Saint Mark* (1963). Philadelphia: Westminster, 1977.

Pesch, R. *Das Markusevangelium.* 2 vols. Freiburg—Basel
—Vienna: Herder, 1976, 1977.

Schmid, J. *The Gospel According to Mark.* Cork, Ireland:
Mercier, 1968; New York: Alba House, 1969.

*Schweizer, E. *The Good News According to Mark.* Richmond, VA: John Knox, 1970.

*Taylor, V. *The Gospel According to St. Mark: The Greek
Text with Introduction, Notes and Indexes.* 2nd ed.
1966. Grand Rapids: Baker, 1981.

29
Mark: Studies

Achtemeier, P. J. *Mark*. Philadelphia: Fortress, 1975.

Best, E. *Following Jesus. Discipleship in the Gospel of Mark.* Sheffield, UK: JSOT Press, 1981.

*_____. *Mark: The Gospel as Story*. Edinburgh: Clark, 1983.

_____. *The Temptation and the Passion: The Markan Soteriology.* New York—London: Cambridge University Press, 1965.

Blevins, J. L. *The Messianic Secret in Markan Research.* Washington, DC: University Press of America, 1981.

Dewey, J. *Markan Public Debate. Literary Technique, Concentric Structure, and Theology in Mark 2:1—3:6.* Chico: Scholars Press, 1980.

Donahue, J. R. "Jesus as the Parable of God in the Gospel of Mark." *Interpretation* 32 (1978) 369-86.

——————. *The Theology and Setting of Discipleship in the Gospel of Mark.* Milwaukee: Marquette University, 1983.

Humphrey, H. M. *A Bibliography for the Gospel of Mark, 1954—1980.* New York—Toronto: Edwin Mellen Press, 1981.

Kealy, S. *Mark's Gospel: A History of Its Interpretation. From the Beginning until 1979.* New York—Ramsey, NJ: Paulist, 1982.

Kee, H. C. *Community of the New Age.* Philadelphia: Westminster, 1977.

Kelber, W. H. *The Kingdom in Mark. A New Place and a New Time.* Philadelphia: Fortress, 1974.

Kermode, F. *The Genesis of Secrecy. On the Interpretation of Narrative.* Cambridge, MA—London: Harvard University Press, 1979.

Kingsbury, J. D. *The Christology of Mark's Gospel.* Philadelphia: Fortress, 1983.

Kuhn, H.—W. *Ältere Sammlungen im Markusevangelium.* Göttingen: Vandenhoeck & Ruprecht, 1971.

Martin, R. P. *Mark: Evangelist and Theologian.* Exeter, UK: Paternoster Press, 1972; Grand Rapids: Zondervan, 1973.

*Marxsen, W. *Mark the Evangelist. Studies on the Redaction History of the Gospel.* Nashville—New York: Abingdon, 1969.

Meye, R. P. *Jesus and the Twelve. Discipleship and Revelation in Mark's Gospel.* Grand Rapids: Eerdmans, 1968.

Quesnell, Q. *The Mind of Mark. Interpretation and Method through the Exegesis of Mark 6, 52.* Rome: Biblical Institute Press, 1969.

Rhoads, D. and D. Michie. *Mark as Story. An Introduction to the Narrative of a Gospel.* Philadelphia: Fortress, 1982.

Robbins, V. K. *Jesus the Teacher.* Philadelphia: Fortress, 1984.

Robinson, J. M. *The Problem of History in Mark and Other Marcan Studies.* Philadelphia: Fortress, 1982.

Stein, R. H. "The Proper Methodology for Ascertaining a Markan Redaction History." *Novum Testamentum* 13 (1971) 181-98.

Stock, A. *Call to Discipleship: A Literary Study of Mark's Gospel.* Wilmington: Michael Glazier, 1982.

Tannehill, R. C. "The Disciples in Mark: The Function of a Narrative Role." *Journal of Religion* 57 (1977) 386-405.

Tuckett, C. M., ed. *The Messianic Secret.* Philadelphia: Fortress, 1983; London: S.P.C.K.

Trocmé, E. *The Formation of the Gospel According to Mark.* Philadelphia: Westminster, 1975.

Weeden, T. J. *Mark—Traditions in Conflict.* Philadelphia: Fortress, 1971.

30
Luke: Commentaries

Caird, G. B. *St. Luke.* Philadelphia: Westminster, 1978.

Creed, J. M. *The Gospel According to St. Luke. The Greek Text, with Introduction, Notes and Indices.* London: Macmillan, 1930.

Danker, F. W. *Jesus and the New Age According to St. Luke: A Commentary on the Third Gospel.* St. Louis: Clayton, 1972.

Ernst, J. *Das Evangelium nach Lukas: Übersetzt und erklärt.* Regensburg: F. Pustet, 1977.

*Fitzmyer, J. A. *The Gospel According to Luke. Introduction, Translation, and Notes.* 2 vols. Garden City, NY: Doubleday, 1981, 1985.

Kealy, S. P. *The Gospel of Luke.* Denville, NJ: Dimension, 1979.

LaVerdiere, E. *Luke.* Wilmington: Michael Glazier, 1980.

*Marshall, I. H. *The Gospel of Luke. A Commentary on the Greek Text.* Grand Rapids: Eerdmans, 1978.

Plummer, A. *A Critical and Exegetical Commentary on the Gospel According to St. Luke.* 5th ed. Edinburgh: Clark, 1922.

Schneider, G. *Das Evangelium nach Lukas.* 2 vols. Gütersloh: Mohn, 1977.

Schürmann, H. *Das Lukasevangelium: Kommentar zur Kap. 1, 1-9, 50.* 2nd rev. ed. Freiburg: Herder, 1982.

*Schweizer, E. *The Good News According to Luke.* Atlanta: John Knox, 1984.

31
Luke: Studies
(see §§ 43, 44)

Bovon, F. *Luc le théologien. Vingt-cinq ans de recherches (1950-1975).* Neuchâtel—Paris: Delachaux & Niestlé, 1978.

Brown, S. *Apostasy and Perseverance in the Theology of Luke.* Rome: Biblical Institute Press, 1969.

Cadbury, H. J. *The Making of Luke-Acts.* London: S.P.C.K., 1958; Naperville, IL: Allenson.

Cassidy, R. J. *Jesus, Politics, and Society: A Study of Luke's Gospel.* Maryknoll, NY: Orbis, 1978.

_____ and P. J. Scharper, eds. *Political Issues in Luke—Acts.* Maryknoll, NY: Orbis Books, 1983.

*Conzelmann, H. *The Theology of St. Luke* (1960). Philadelphia: Fortress, 1982.

Drury, J. *Tradition and Design in Luke's Gospel: A Study in Early Christian Historiography.* Atlanta: John Knox, 1976.

Egelkraut, H. L. *Jesus' Mission to Jerusalem: A Redaction-Critical Study of the Travel Narrative in the Gospel of Luke, Lk 9:51-19:48.* Frankfurt: P. Lang, 1976; Bern: H. Lang.

Flender, H. *St. Luke: Theologian of Redemptive History.* Philadelphia: Fortress, 1967.

Franklin, E. *Christ the Lord. A Study in the Purpose and Theology of Luke.* Philadelphia: Westminster, 1976.

Gill, D. "Observations on the Lukan Travel Narrative and Some Related Passages." *Harvard Theological Review* 63 (1970) 199-221.

Jervell, J. *Luke and the People of God. A New Look at Luke—Acts.* Minneapolis: Augsburg, 1972.

Johnson, L. T. *The Literary Function of Possessions in Luke—Acts.* Missoula: Scholars, 1977.

Juel, D. *Luke—Acts: The Promise of History.* Atlanta: John Knox, 1983.

Karris, R. J. *Luke: Artist and Theologian. Luke's Passion Account as Literature.* New York—Mahwah, NJ—Toronto: Paulist, 1985.

_____. *What Are They Saying About Luke and Acts? A Theology of the Faithful God.* New York: Paulist, 1979.

Keck, L. E. and J. L. Martyn, eds. *Studies in Luke—Acts* (1966). Philadelphia: Fortress, 1980.

Lohfink, G. *Die Himmelfahrt Jesu. Untersuchungen zu den Himmelfahrts- und Erhöhungstexten bei Lukas.* Munich: Kösel, 1971.

_____. *Die Sammlung Israels: Eine Untersuchung zur lukanischen Ekklesiologie.* Munich: Kösel, 1975.

Maddox, R. *The Purpose of Luke—Acts.* Göttingen: Vandenhoeck & Ruprecht, 1982.

Marshall, I. H. *Luke: Historian and Theologian.* Exeter, UK: Paternoster, 1970; Grand Rapids: Eerdmans, 1971.

Minear, P. S. *To Heal and to Reveal: The Prophetic Vocation According to Luke.* New York: Seabury, 1976.

Navone, J. *Themes of St. Luke.* Rome: Gregorian University Press, 1970.

Néirynck, F., ed. *L'Evangile de Luc: problèmes littéraires et théologiques.* Gembloux: Duculot, 1973.

O'Toole, R. F. *The Unity of Luke's Theology. An Analysis of Luke—Acts.* Wilmington: Michael Glazier, 1984.

Pilgrim, W. E. *Good News to the Poor. Wealth and Poverty in Luke—Acts.* Minneapolis: Augsburg, 1981.

*Richard, E. "Luke—Writer, Theologian, Historian: Research and Orientation of the 1970's." *Biblical Theology Bulletin* 13 (1983) 3-15.

Schweizer, E. *Luke: A Challenge to Present Theology.* Atlanta: John Knox, 1982.

Talbert, C. H. *Literary Patterns, Theological Themes, and the Genre of Luke—Acts.* Missoula: Scholars, 1974.

_____. *Reading Luke. A Literary and Theological Commentary on the Third Gospel.* New York: Crossroad, 1982.

_____, ed. *Luke—Acts. New Perspectives from the Society of Biblical Literature Seminar.* New York: Crossroad, 1984.

_____, ed. *Perspectives on Luke—Acts.* Danville, VA: Association of Baptist Professors of Religion, 1978; Edinburgh: Clark.

Tiede, D. L. *Prophecy and History in Luke-Acts.* Philadelphia: Fortress, 1980.

Wilson, S. G. *The Gentiles and the Gentile Mission in Luke-Acts.* New York: Cambridge University Press, 1973.

_____. *Luke and the Law.* Cambridge, UK—London—New York: Cambridge University Press, 1984.

32
Infancy Narratives

Brown, R. E. *An Adult Christ at Christmas. Essays on the Three Biblical Christmas Stories.* Collegeville, MN: Liturgical Press, 1978.

*_____. *The Birth of the Messiah. A Commentary on the Infancy Narratives in Matthew and Luke.* Garden City, NY: Doubleday, 1977.

de Jonge, H. J. "Sonship, Wisdom, Infancy: Luke ii. 41-51a." *New Testament Studies* 24 (1978) 317-54.

Johnson, M. D. *The Purpose of the Biblical Genealogies. With Special Reference to the Setting of the Genealogies of Jesus.* New York: Cambridge University Press, 1969.

Laurentin, R. *Les Evangiles de l'Enfance du Christ. Vérité de Noël au-delà des mythes. Exégèse et sémiotique, historicité et théologie.* Paris: Desclée—Desclée de Brouwer, 1982.

Nolan, B. M. *The Royal Son of God. The Christology of Matthew 1—2 in the Setting of the Gospels.* Fribourg: Editions Universitaires, 1979; Göttingen: Vandenhoeck & Ruprecht.

Perrot, C. "Les récits d'enfance dans la Haggada anterieure au IIe siècle de notre ère." *Recherches de Science Religieuse* 55 (1967) 481-518.

Soares-Prabhu, G. M. *The Formula Quotations in the Infancy Narrative of Matthew. An Enquiry into the Tradition History of Mt 1—2.* Rome: Biblical Institute Press, 1976.

Stendahl, K. "Quis et Unde? An Analysis of Mt 1—2." *Judentum, Urchristentum, Kirche. Festschrift für Joachim Jeremias*, ed. W. Eltester. Berlin: Töpelmann, 1960. Pp. 95-105.

Tannehill, R. C. "The Magnificat as Poem." *Journal of Biblical Literature* 93 (1974) 263-75.

33
Virginal Conception

Boslooper, T. *The Virgin Birth*. Philadelphia: Westminster, 1962.

*Brown, R. E. *The Virginal Conception and Bodily Resurrection of Jesus*. Paramus, NJ: Paulist, 1973.

Fitzmyer, J. A. "The Virginal Conception of Jesus in the New Testament." *Theological Studies* 34 (1973) 541-75.

Grelot, P. "La naissance d'Isaac et celle de Jésus. Sur une interprétation 'mythologique' de la conception virginale." *Nouvelle Revue Théologique* 104 (1972) 462-87, 561-85.

Miguens, M. "Mary, A Virgin? Alleged Silence in the New Testament." *Marian Studies* 26 (1975) 26-179; also published as a book: *The Virgin Birth. An Evaluation of Scriptural Evidence* (Westminster, MD: Christian Classics, 1975).

Saliba, J. A. "The Virgin-Birth Debate in Anthropological Literature: A Critical Assessment." *Theological Studies* 36 (1975) 428-54.

von Campenhausen, H. *The Virgin Birth in the Theology of the Ancient Church*. Naperville, IL: Allenson, 1964.

34
Jesus
(see § 69-70)

Anderson, H. *Jesus and Christian Origins. A Commentary on Modern Viewpoints.* New York: Oxford University Press, 1964.

*Bornkamm, G. *Jesus of Nazareth.* London: Hodder & Stoughton, 1960; New York: Harper.

Braun, H. *Jesus of Nazareth. The Man and His Time.* Philadelphia: Fortress, 1979.

Brown, R. E. "How Much Did Jesus Know?—A Survey of the Biblical Evidence." *Catholic Biblical Quarterly* 29 (1967) 315-45.

Bultmann, R. *Jesus and the Word* (1935). Edinburgh: Clark, 1980.

Conzelmann, H. *Jesus.* Philadelphia: Fortress, 1973.

Dalman, G. *Jesus—Jeshua. Studies in the Gospels* (1929). New York: Ktav, 1971.

Dodd, C. H. *The Founder of Christianity.* New York—London: Macmillan, 1970.

Duling, D. C. *Jesus Christ Through History*. New York: Harcourt Brace Jovanovich, 1979.

Fuchs, E. *Studies of the Historical Jesus*. Naperville, IL: Allenson, 1964.

Harvey, A. E. *Jesus and the Constraints of History*. Philadelphia: Westminster, 1982.

Hengel, M. *The Charismatic Leader and His Followers*. New York: Crossroad, 1981.

Keck, L. E. *A Future for the Historical Jesus. The Place of Jesus in Preaching and Theology* (1971). Philadelphia: Fortress, 1981.

Kee, H. C. *Jesus in History. An Approach to the Study of the Gospels*. 2nd ed. New York: Harcourt Brace Jovanovich, 1977.

Perrot, C. *Jésus et l'histoire*. Tournai: Desclée, 1979.

Reumann, J. *Jesus in the Church's Gospels: Modern Scholarship and the Earliest Sources*. Philadelphia: Fortress, 1968.

Riches, J. *Jesus and the Transformation of Judaism*. London: Darton, Longman & Todd, 1980.

Robinson, J. M. *A New Quest of the Historical Jesus and Other Essays*. Philadelphia: Fortress, 1983.

*Sanders, E. P. *Jesus and Judaism*. Philadelphia: Fortress, 1985.

Schweitzer, A. *The Quest of the Historical Jesus. A Critical Study of its Progress from Reimarus to Wrede.* New York: Macmillan, 1961.

Stauffer, E. *Jesus and His Story.* New York: Knopf, 1960.

Vermes, G. *Jesus and the World of Judaism.* Philadelphia: Fortress, 1984.

_____. *Jesus the Jew. A Historian's Reading of the Gospels.* New York: Macmillan, 1974.

Zahrnt, H. *The Historical Jesus.* New York—Evanston: Harper & Row, 1963.

35
Jesus' Teachings —
esp. the Kingdom of God
(see §§ 72, 93)

Chilton, B. D. *God in Strength. Jesus' Announcement of the Kingdom.* Linz: SNTU, 1979.

*_____, ed. *The Kingdom of God in the Teaching of Jesus.* Philadelphia: Fortress, 1984; London: S.P.C.K.

Glasson, T. F. *Jesus and the End of the World.* Edinburgh: St. Andrew Press, 1980.

Gray, J. *The Biblical Doctrine of the Reign of God.* Edinburgh: Clark, 1979.

Hartman, L. *Prophecy Interpreted. The Formation of Some Jewish Apocalyptic Texts and of the Eschatological Discourse Mark 13 par.* Lund: C.W.K. Gleerup, 1966.

Hiers, R. H. *The Historical Jesus and the Kingdom of God. Present and Future in the Message and Ministry of Jesus.* Gainesville: University of Florida Press, 1973.

_____. *Jesus and the Future. Unresolved Questions for Understanding and Faith.* Atlanta: John Knox, 1981.

_____. *The Kingdom of God in the Synoptic Tradition.* Gainesville: University of Florida Press, 1970.

Jeremias, J. *Jesus' Promise to the Nations.* London: SCM, 1958; Philadelphia: Fortress, 1982.

*_____. *New Testament Theology. The Proclamation of Jesus.* New York: Scribner's, 1971.

_____. *The Prayers of Jesus.* Naperville, IL: Allenson, 1967.

Kümmel, W. G. *Promise and Fulfillment. The Eschatological Message of Jesus.* London: SCM, 1957.

Künzi, M. *Das Naherwartungslogion Matthäus 10, 23. Geschichte seiner Auslegung.* Tübingen: Mohr-Siebeck, 1970.

Ladd, G. E. *The Presence of the Future. The Eschatology of Biblical Realism.* Grand Rapids: Eerdmans, 1974.

Lambrecht, J. *Die Redaktion der Markus—Apokalypse. Literarische Analyse und Strukturuntersuchung.* Rome: Biblical Institute Press, 1967.

Lundström, G. *The Kingdom of God in the Teaching of Jesus. A History of Interpretation from the Last Decades of the Nineteenth Century to the Present Day.* Richmond, VA: John Knox, 1963.

Manson, T. W. *The Teaching of Jesus. Studies in its Form and Content* (1935). New York—London: Cambridge University Press, 1963.

Meyer, B. F. *The Aims of Jesus.* London: SCM, 1979.

Perrin, N. *Jesus and the Language of the Kingdom. Symbol and Metaphor in New Testament Interpretation.* Philadelphia: Fortress, 1976.

_____. *The Kingdom of God in the Teaching of Jesus.* Philadelphia: Westminster, 1963.

*_____. *Rediscovering the Teaching of Jesus.* New York—Evanston: Harper & Row, 1967.

Pesch, R. *Naherwartungen. Tradition und Redaktion in Mk 13.* Düsseldorf: Patmos, 1968.

Schlosser, J. *Règne de Dieu dans les dits de Jésus.* 2 vols. Paris: Gabalda, 1980.

Stein, R. H. *The Method and Message of Jesus' Teachings.* Philadelphia: Westminster, 1978.

Weiss, J. *Jesus' Proclamation of the Kingdom of God.* Philadelphia: Fortress, 1971.

36
Parables

Boucher, M. *The Mysterious Parable. A Literary Study.* Washington, DC: Catholic Biblical Association, 1977.

_____. *The Parables.* Wilmington: Michael Glazier, 1981.

Borsch, F. H. *God's Parable.* Philadelphia: Westminster, 1976.

Carlston, C. E. *The Parables of the Triple Tradition.* Philadelphia: Fortress, 1975.

Crossan, J. D. *In Parables. The Challenge of the Historical Jesus.* New York—London: Harper & Row, 1973.

*Dodd, C. H. *The Parables of the Kingdom.* Rev. ed. New York: Scribner's, 1965.

Funk, R. W. *Parables and Presence. Forms of the New Testament Tradition.* Philadelphia: Fortress, 1982.

Harnisch, W., ed. *Gleichnisse Jesu. Positionen der Auslegung von Adolf Jülicher bis zur Formgeschichte.* Darmstadt: Wissenschaftliche Buchgesellschaft, 1982.

_____. *Die neutestamentliche Gleichnisforschung im Horizont von Hermeneutik und Literaturwissenschaft.* Darmstadt: Wissenschaftliche Buchgesellschaft, 1982.

*Jeremias, J. *The Parables of Jesus.* Rev. ed. New York: Scribner's, 1963.

Kingsbury, J. D. *The Parables of Jesus in Matthew 13. A Study in Redaction-Criticism.* Richmond, VA: Knox, 1969.

Kissinger, W. S. *The Parables of Jesus. A History of Interpretation and Bibliography.* Metuchen, NJ—London: Scarecrow Press, 1979.

Klauck, H.—J. *Allegorie und Allegorese in synoptischen Gleichnistexten.* Münster: Aschendorff, 1978.

Lambrecht, J. *Once More Astonished. The Parables of Jesus.* New York: Crossroad, 1981.

Linnemann, E. *Jesus of the Parables. Introduction and Exposition.* New York—Evanston, IL: Harper & Row, 1966.

McFague Te Selle, S. *Speaking in Parables. A Study in Metaphor and Theology.* Philadelphia: Fortress, 1975.

Perkins, P. *Hearing the Parables of Jesus.* New York-Ramsey, NJ: Paulist, 1981.

Scott, B. B. *Jesus, Symbol-Maker for the Kingdom.* Philadelphia: Fortress, 1981.

Stein, R. H. *An Introduction to the Parables of Jesus.* Philadelphia: Westminster, 1981.

Tolbert, M. A. *Perspectives on the Parables. An Approach to Multiple Interpretations.* Philadelphia: Fortress, 1979.

Via, D. O. *The Parables. Their Literary and Existential Dimension.* Philadelphia: Fortress, 1967.

Wilder, A. N. *Jesus' Parables and the War of Myths. Essays on Imagination in the Scripture.* Philadelphia: Fortress, 1982.

37
Miracles

Brown, C. *Miracles and the Critical Mind*. Grand Rapids: Eerdmans, 1984; Exeter, UK: Paternoster.

Fridrichsen, A. *The Problem of Miracle in Primitive Christianity*. Minneapolis: Augsburg, 1972.

Fuller, R. H. *Interpreting the Miracles*. Philadelphia: Westminster, 1963.

*Kee, H. C. *Miracle in the Early Christian World. A Study in Sociohistorical Method*. New Haven—London: Yale University Press, 1983.

Léon-Dufour, X., ed. *Les Miracles de Jésus selon le Nouveau Testament*. Paris: Seuil, 1977.

Moule, C. F. D., ed. *Miracles. Cambridge Studies in their Philosophy and History*. London: Mowbray, 1965.

Mussner, F. *The Miracles of Jesus. An Introduction*. Notre Dame, IN: University of Notre Dame Press, 1968.

Remus, H. *Pagan-Christian Conflict over Miracle in the Second Century.* Cambridge, MA: Philadelphia Patristic Foundation, 1983.

Suhl, A., ed. *Der Wunderbegriff im Neuen Testament.* Darmstadt: Wissenschaftliche Buchgesellschaft, 1980.

*Theissen, G. *The Miracle Stories of the Early Christian Tradition.* Philadelphia: Fortress, 1983.

38
Various Topics

Banks, R. *Jesus and the Law in the Synoptic Tradition.* London—New York—Melbourne: Cambridge University Press, 1975.

Berger, K. *Die Amen-Worte Jesu. Eine Untersuchung zum Problem der Legitimation in apokalyptischer Rede.* Berlin: de Gruyter, 1970.

Boring, M. E. *Sayings of the Risen Jesus. Christian Prophecy in the Synoptic Tradition.* Cambridge, UK—London—New York: Cambridge University Press, 1982.

Carmignac, J. *Recherches sur le "Notre Père."* Paris: Letouzey & Ané, 1969.

Crossan, J. D. *In Fragments. The Aphorisms of Jesus.* San Francisco: Harper & Row, 1983.

Dorneich, M., ed. *Vater-Unser Bibliographie—The Lord's Prayer, A Bibliography.* Freiburg: Herder, 1982.

Dupont, J. *Les Béatitudes.* 3 vols. Paris: Gabalda, 1958, 1969, 1973.

Gaston, L. *No Stone on Another. Studies in the Significance of the Fall of Jerusalem in the Synoptic Gospels.* Leiden: Brill, 1970.

Hasler, V. *Amen. Redaktionsgeschichtliche Untersuchung zur Einführungsformel der Herrenworte "Wahrlich ich sage euch."* Zurich—Stuttgart: Gotthelf, 1969.

Hultgren, A. J. *Jesus and His Adversaries. The Form and Function of the Conflict Stories in the Synoptic Tradition.* Minnepolis: Augsburg, 1979.

Kelber, W. H. *The Oral and the Written Gospel. The Hermeneutics of Speaking and Writing in the Synoptic Tradition, Mark, Paul, and Q.* Philadelphia: Fortress, 1983.

Kissinger, W. *The Sermon on the Mount: A History of Interpretation and Bibliography.* Metuchen, NJ: Scarecrow Press, 1975.

Lambrecht, J. *The Sermon on the Mount: Proclamation and Exhortation.* Wilmington: Michael Glazier, 1985.

*Mays, J. L., ed. *Interpreting the Gospels.* Philadelphia: Fortress, 1981.

*Rohde, J. *Rediscovering the Teaching of the Evangelists.* Philadelphia: Westminster, 1969.

Schütz, R. *Johannes der Täufer.* Zurich—Stuttgart: Zwingli-Verlag, 1967.

Talbert, C. H. *What Is a Gospel? The Genre of the Canonical Gospels.* Philadelphia: Fortress, 1977.

Wink, W. *John the Baptist in the Gospel Tradition.* New York: Cambridge University Press, 1968.

Wuellner, W. H. *The Meaning of "Fishers of Men."* Philadelphia: Westminster, 1967.

39
Passion Narratives
(see § 76)

Benoit, P. *The Passion and Resurrection of Jesus Christ.* New York: Herder & Herder, 1969; London: Darton, Longman & Todd.

Blinzler, J. *The Trial of Jesus. The Jewish and Roman Proceedings against Jesus Christ described and assessed from the Oldest Accounts.* Westminster, MD: Newman, 1959.

Brandon, S. G. F. *The Trial of Jesus of Nazareth.* New York: Stein & Day, 1968.

Brown, R. E. "Brief Observations on the Shroud of Turin." *Biblical Theology Bulletin* 14 (1984) 145-48.

Dinkler, E. "Comments on the History of the Symbol of the Cross." *Journal of Theology and Church* 1 (1965) 124-46.

Donahue, J. R. *Are You the Christ? The Trial Narrative in the Gospel of Mark.* Cambridge, MA: Society of Biblical Literature, 1973.

Fitzmyer, J. A. "Crucifixion in Ancient Palestine, Qumran Literature, and the New Testament." *Catholic Biblical Quarterly* 40 (1978) 493-513.

Gordis, R., ed. *The Trial of Jesus in the Light of History*, in *Judaism* 20 (1971) 6-74 (Articles by H. Cohn, M. S. Enslin, D. Flusser, R. M. Grant, S. F. G. Brandon, J. Blinzler, G. S. Sloyan, and S. Sandmel.)

*Hengel, M. *Crucifixion. In the ancient world and the folly of the message of the cross.* Philadelphia: Fortress, 1977.

Jaubert, A. *The Date of the Last Supper.* Staten Island, NY: Alba House, 1965.

Juel, D. *Messiah and Temple. The Trial of Jesus in the Gospel of Mark.* Missoula: Scholars, 1977.

Kelber, W. H., ed. *The Passion in Mark. Studies on Mark 14-16.* Philadelphia: Fortress, 1976.

Limbeck, M., ed. *Redaktion und Theologie des Passionsberichtes nach den Synoptikern.* Darmstadt: Wissenschaftliche Buchgesellschaft, 1981.

Lohfink, G. *The Last Day of Jesus. An Enriching Portrayal of the Passion.* Notre Dame, IN: Ave Maria Press, 1984.

Lohse, E. *History of the Suffering and Death of Jesus.* Philadelphia: Fortress, 1967.

Marin, L. *The Semiotics of the Passion Narrative. Topics and Figures.* Pittsburgh, PA: Pickwick, 1980.

Moo, D. J. *The Old Testament in the Gospel Passion Narrative*. Sheffield, UK: Almond Press, 1983.

E. Rivkin, *What Crucified Jesus?* Nashville: Abingdon, 1984.

Senior, D. P. *The Passion Narrative According to Matthew. A Redactional Study*. Gembloux: Duculot, 1975.

*_____. *The Passion of Jesus in the Gospel of Mark*. Wilmington: Michael Glazier, 1984.

*_____. *The Passion of Jesus in the Gospel of Matthew*. Wilmington: Michael Glazier, 1985.

Sloyan, G. S. *Jesus on Trial. The Development of the Passion Narratives and Their Historical and Ecumenical Implications*. Philadelphia: Fortress, 1973.

Stanley, D. M. *Jesus in Gethsemane*. New York—Ramsey, NJ: Paulist, 1980.

Taylor, V. *The Passion Narrative of St. Luke. A Critical and Historical Investigation*. New York—London: Cambridge University Press, 1972.

Tzaferis, V. "Crucifixion—The Archaeological Evidence." *Biblical Archaeology Review* 11 (1985) 44-53.

Wilson, W. R. *The Execution of Jesus. A Judicial, Literary and Historical Investigation*. New York: Scribner's, 1970.

Winter, P. *On the Trial of Jesus*. Berlin: de Gruyter, 1961.

40
Resurrection

Alsup, J. E. *The Post-Resurrection Appearance Stories of the Gospel Tradition. A History-of-Tradition Analysis with Text-Synopsis.* Stuttgart: Calwer, 1975.

Bode, E. L. *The First Easter Morning. The Gospel Accounts of the Women's Visit to the Tomb of Jesus.* Rome: Biblical Institute Press, 1970.

Brown, R. E. *The Virginal Conception and Bodily Resurrection of Jesus.* Paramus, NJ: Paulist, 1973.

Dhanis, E., ed. *Resurrexit. Actes du symposium sur la résurrection de Jésus (Rome 1970).* Vatican City: Libreria Editrice Vaticana, 1974.

Durrwell, F. X. *The Resurrection. A Biblical Study.* New York: Sheed and Ward, 1960.

Evans, C. F. *Resurrection and the New Testament.* Naperville, IL: Allenson, 1970.

Fuller, R. H. *The Formation of the Resurrection Narratives.* New York: Macmillan, 1971.

Léon-Dufour, X. *Resurrection and the Message of Easter.* New York: Holt, Rinehart & Winston, 1975.

Marxsen, W. *The Resurrection of Jesus of Nazareth.* Philadelphia: Fortress, 1970.

O'Collins, G. *The Resurrection of Jesus Christ.* Valley Forge, PA: Judson, 1973.

*Perkins, P. *Resurrection: New Testament Witness and Contemporary Reflection.* Garden City, NY: Doubleday, 1984.

Perrin, N. *The Resurrection According to Matthew, Mark, and Luke.* Philadelphia: Fortress, 1977.

Rochais, G. *Les récits de résurrection des morts dans le Nouveau Testament.* Cambridge, UK—London—New York: Cambridge University Press, 1981.

Wilckens, U. *Resurrection. Biblical Testimony to the Resurrection: An Historical Examination and Explanation.* Atlanta: John Knox, 1978.

41
John: Commentaries
(see § 62)

Barrett, C. K. *The Gospel according to St. John. An Intro-duction with Commentary and Notes on the Greek Text.* 2nd ed. Philadelphia: Westminster, 1978.

Bernard, J. H. *A Critical and Exegetical Commentary on the Gospel according to St. John.* 2 vols. Edinburgh: Clark, 1928.

Boismard, M.—E. and A. Lamouille. *Synopse des quatres Evangiles en français. Tome III: L'Evangile de Jean.* Paris: Cerf, 1977.

*Brown, R. E. *The Gospel According to John. Introduction, Translation, and Notes.* 2 vols. New York: Doubleday, 1966, 1970.

Bruce, F. F. *The Gospel of John. Introduction, Exposition and Notes.* Grand Rapids: Eerdmans, 1983.

*Bultmann, R. *The Gospel of John. A Commentary.* Philadelphia: Westminster, 1971.

Haenchen, E. *John. A Commentary on the Gospel of John.* 2 vols. Philadelphia: Fortress, 1984.

Lagrange, M.—J. *Evangile selon Saint Jean.* 8th ed. Paris: Gabalda, 1948.

Lightfoot, R. H. *St. John's Gospel: A Commentary.* Oxford: Clarendon Press, 1956.

Lindars, B. *The Gospel of John.* Greenwood, SC: Attic Press, 1972; London: Oliphants.

Marsh, J. *Saint John.* Philadelphia: Westminster, 1978.

McPolin, J. *John.* Rev. ed. Wilmington: Michael Glazier, 1982.

Morris, L. *The Gospel According to John.* Grand Rapids: Eerdmans, 1971.

Sanders, J. N. *A Commentary on the Gospel According to St. John.* New York—Evanston, IL: Harper & Row, 1969.

*Schnackenburg, R. *The Gospel According to St. John.* 3 vols. New York: Crossroad, 1968/80, 1979/81, 1982.

42
John: Studies

Appold, M. L. *The Oneness Motif in the Fourth Gospel.
Motif Analysis and Exegetical Probe into the Theology
of John.* Tübingen: Mohr-Siebeck, 1976.

Borgen, P. *Bread from Heaven. An Exegetical Study of the
Concept of Manna in the Gospel of John and the
Writings of Philo.* Leiden: Brill, 1965.

Braun, F.—M. *Jean le théologien.* 3 vols. Paris: Gabalda,
1959, 1964, 1966.

*Brown, R. E. *The Community of the Beloved Disciple.* New
York—Ramsey, NJ—Toronto: Paulist, 1979.

Charlesworth, J. H., ed. *John and Qumran.* London: Chap-
man, 1972.

Cullmann, O. *The Johannine Circle.* Philadelphia: Westminster, 1976.

Culpepper, R. A. *Anatomy of the Fourth Gospel. A Study
in Literary Design.* Philadelphia: Fortress, 1983.

_____. *The Johannine School: An Evaluation of the Johannine-School Hypothesis Based on an Investigation of the Nature of Ancient Schools.* Missoula: Scholars, 1975.

de la Potterie, I. *La vérité dans Saint Jean.* 2 vols. Rome: Biblical Institute Press, 1977.

Dodd, C. H. *The Interpretation of the Fourth Gospel.* New York—London: Cambridge University Press, 1953.

_____. *Historical Tradition in the Fourth Gospel.* New York—London: Cambridge University Press, 1963.

Duprez, A. *Jesus et les dieux guérisseurs. A propos de Jean V.* Paris: Gabalda, 1970.

Fortna, R. T. *The Gospel of Signs. A Reconstruction of the Narrative Source Underlying the Fourth Gospel.* New York—London: Cambridge University Press, 1970.

Johnston, G. *The Spirit-Paraclete in the Gospel of John.* New York—London: Cambridge University Press, 1970.

Käsemann, E. *The Testament of Jesus. A Study of the Gospel of John in the Light of Chapter 17.* Philadelphia: Fortress, 1968.

*Kysar, R. *The Fourth Evangelist and His Gospel. An Examnation of Contemporary Scholarship.* Minneapolis: Augsburg, 1975.

_____. *John the Maverick Gospel.* Atlanta: John Knox, 1976.

Malatesta, E. *St. John's Gospel 1920-1965. A Cumulative and Classified Bibliography of Books and Periodical Literature on the Fourth Gospel.* Rome: Pontifical Biblical Institute, 1967.

Martyn, J. L. *History & Theology in the Fourth Gospel.* 2nd rev. ed. Nashville: Abingdon, 1979.

Meeks, W. A. "The Man from Heaven in Johannine Sectarianism." *Journal of Biblical Literature* 91 (1972) 44-72.

_____ *The Prophet-King. Moses Traditions and the Johannine Christology.* Leiden: Brill, 1967.

Moloney, F. J. *The Johannine Son of Man.* 2nd ed. Rome: Libreria Ateneo Salesiano, 1978.

Nicol, W. *The Semeia in the Fourth Gospel. Tradition and Redaction.* Leiden: Brill, 1972.

Painter, J. *John: Witness and Theologian.* Rev. ed. London: S.P.C.K., 1979.

Smalley. S. S. *John: Evangelist and Interpreter.* Exeter, UK: Paternoster, 1978.

Smith, D. M. *The Composition and Order of the Fourth Gospel. Bultmann's Literary Theory.* New Haven, CT—London: Yale University Press, 1965.

Taylor, M. J., ed. *A Companion to John. Readings in Johannine Theology (John's Gospel and Epistles).* New York: Alba House, 1977.

Wead, D. W. *The Literary Devices in John's Gospel.* Basel: F. Reinhardt, 1970.

43
Acts: Commentaries

Bruce, F. F. *The Acts of the Apostles*. Grand Rapids: Eerdmans, 1953.

Crowe, J. *The Acts*. Wilmington: Michael Glazier, 1979.

Foakes Jackson, F. J. and K. Lake, eds. *The Beginnings of Christianity* (1920-33). 5 vols. Grand Rapids: Baker, 1979.

*Haenchen, E. *The Acts of the Apostles*. Philadelphia: Westminster, 1971.

*Marshall, I. *The Acts of the Apostles. An Introduction and Commentary*. Grand Rapids: Eerdmans. 1980.

Munck, J. *The Acts of the Apostles*. Garden City, NY: Doubleday, 1967.

Schneider, G. *Die Apostelgeschichte*. 2 vols. Freiburg—Basel—Vienna: Herder, 1980, 1982.

Williams, C. S. C. *A Commentary on the Acts of the Apostles*. 2nd ed. New York: Harper & Row, 1964.

44
Acts: Studies
(see §§ 30-31, 45)

Dibelius, M. *Studies in the Acts of the Apostles* (1956). London: SCM, 1973.

Dupont, J. *Etudes sur les Actes des Apôtres.* Paris: Cerf, 1967.

——————. *Nouvelles études sur les Actes des Apôtres.* Paris: Cerf, 1984.

——————. *The Salvation of the Gentiles. Essays on the Acts of the Apostles.* New York—Ramsey, NJ—Toronto: Paulist, 1979.

——————. *The Sources of the Acts.* New York: Herder & Herder, 1964.

*Gasque, W. W. *A History of the Criticism of the Acts of the Apostles.* Grand Rapids: Eerdmans, 1975.

*Hengel, M. *Acts and the History of Earliest Christianity.* London: SCM, 1979; Philadelphia: Fortress, 1980.

Kilgallen, J. *The Stephen Speech. A Literary and Redactional Study of Acts 7, 2-53.* Rome: Biblical Institute Press, 1976.

Kremer, J., ed. *Les Actes des Apôtres. Traditions, rédaction, théologie.* Gembloux: Duculot, 1979; Louvain: Leuven University Press.

Lohfink, G. *The Conversion of St. Paul: Narrative and History in Acts.* Chicago: Franciscan Herald Press, 1976.

Mattill, A. J. and M. B. Mattill, eds. *A Classified Bibliography of Literature on the Acts of the Apostles.* Leiden: Brill, 1966.

O'Neill, J. C. *The Theology of Acts in Its Historical Setting.* London: S.P.C.K., 1970.

Plümacher, E. *Lukas als hellenistischer Schriftsteller. Studien zur Apostelgeschichte.* Göttingen: Vandenhoeck & Ruprecht, 1972.

Radl, W. *Paulus und Jesus im lukanischen Doppelwerk: Untersuchungen zu Parallelmotiven im Lukasevangelium und in der Apostelgeschichte.* Bern: Lang, 1975.

Richard, E. *Acts 6:1-8:4: The Author's Method of Composition.* Missoula: Scholars, 1978.

Walaskay, P. W. *"And so we came to Rome." The Political Perspective of St. Luke.* Cambridge, UK—London—New York: Cambridge University Press, 1983.

Wilckens, U. *Die Missionreden der Apostelgeschichte. Form— und traditionsgeschichtliche Untersuchungen.* Neukirchen—Vluyn: Neukirchener, 1961.

Wilcox, M. *The Semitisms of Acts.* New York: Oxford University Press, 1965; Oxford: Clarendon Press.

Zehnle, R. F. *Peter's Pentecost Discourse. Tradition and Lukan Reinterpretation in Peter's Speeches of Acts 2 and 3.* Nashville—New York: Abingdon, 1971.

IV. Epistles

45
Paul

*Bornkamm, G. *Paul.* New York—Evanston, IL: Harper & Row, 1971.

Jewett, R. *A Chronology of Paul's Life.* Philadelphia: Fortress, 1979.

Kim, S. *The Origin of Paul's Gospel.* Tübingen: Mohr-Siebeck, 1981; Grand Rapids: Eerdmans, 1982.

Lüdemann, G. *Paul, Apostle to the Gentiles. Studies in Chronology.* Philadelphia: Fortress, 1984.

McDonald, D. R. *The Legend and the Apostle. The Battle for Paul in Story and Canon.* Philadelphia: Westminster, 1983.

Pagels, E. H. *The Gnostic Paul.* Philadelphia: Fortress, 1975.

Sandmel, S. *The Genius of Paul.* New York: Farrar, Straus and Cudahy, 1958.

Stendahl, K. "The Apostle Paul and the Introspective Conscience of the West." *Harvard Theological Review* 56 (1963) 199-215.

46
Paul's Letters

Doty, W. G. *Letters in Primitive Christianity*. Philadelphia: Fortress, 1973.

Francis, F. O. and J. P. Sampley, eds. *Pauline Parallels*. 2nd ed. Philadelphia: Fortress, 1984.

*Keck, L. E. *Paul and His Letters*. Philadelphia: Fortress, 1979.

_____ and V. P. Furnish. *The Pauline Letters*. Nashville: Abingdon, 1984.

Meeks, W. A., ed. *The Writings of St. Paul*. New York: Norton, 1972.

Metzger, B. M., ed. *Index to Periodical Literature on the Apostle Paul*. Leiden: Brill, 1960; Grand Rapids: Eerdmans.

Patte, D. *Paul's Faith and the Power of the Gospel. A Structural Introduction to the Pauline Letters*. Philadelphia: Fortress, 1983.

Rigaux, B. *The Letters of St. Paul. Modern Studies.* Chicago: Franciscan Herald, 1968.

Roetzel, C. J. *The Letters of Paul. Conversations in Context.* 2nd ed. Atlanta: John Knox, 1982.

Schweitzer, A. *Paul and His Interpreters. A Critical History.* New York: Schocken Books, 1964.

Taylor, M. J., ed. *A Companion to Paul. Readings in Pauline Theology.* New York: Alba House, 1975.

47
Paul's World

Davies, W. D. *Paul and Rabbinic Judaism. Some Rabbinic Elements in Pauline Theology.* 4th ed. Philadelphia: Fortress, 1980.

Hock, R. A. *The Social Context of Paul's Ministry. Tentmaking and Apostleship.* Philadelphia: Fortress, 1980.

*Meeks, W. A. *The First Urban Christians. The Social World of the Apostle Paul.* New Haven—London: Yale University Press, 1983.

Murphy-O'Connor, J., ed. *Paul and Qumran. Studies in New Testament Exegesis.* Chicago: Priory, 1968.

Nock, A. D. *St. Paul* (1938). New York—Evanston, IL: Harper & Row, 1963.

Sanders, E. P. *Paul and Palestinian Judaism. A Comparison of Patterns of Religion.* Philadelphia: Fortress, 1977.

Schoeps, H. J. *Paul. The Theology of the Apostle in the Light of Jewish Religious History.* Philadelphia: Westminster, 1961.

Theissen, G. *The Social Setting of Pauline Christianity. Essays on Corinth.* Philadelphia: Fortress, 1982.

48
Paul's Theology
(see §§ 59, 65-87)

Beker, J. C. *Paul the Apostle. The Triumph of God in Life and Thought*. Philadelphia: Fortress, 1980.

Bouttier, M. *Christianity according to Paul*. Naperville, IL: Allenson, 1966.

Bruce, F. F. *Paul: Apostle of the Heart Set Free*. Grand Rapids: Eerdmans, 1977; Exeter, UK: Paternoster.

Dahl, N. A. *Studies in Paul: Theology for the Early Mission*. Minneapolis: Augsburg, 1977.

Dodd, C. H. *The Meaning of Paul for Today*. London: Collins, 1958.

*Fitzmyer, J. A. *Pauline Theology. A Brief Sketch*. Englewood Cliffs, NJ: Prentice-Hall, 1967.

Giblin, C. H. *In Hope of God's Glory. Pauline Theological Perspectives*. New York: Herder & Herder, 1970.

Käsemann, E. *Perspectives on Paul*. Philadelphia: Fortress, 1971.

Martin, R. P. *Reconciliation. A Study of Paul's Theology.* Atlanta: John Knox, 1981.

Whiteley, D. E. H. *The Theology of St. Paul.* Philadelphia: Fortress, 1964.

Ziesler, J. A. *Pauline Christianity.* Oxford—New York: Oxford University Press, 1983.

49
Romans

Achtemeier, P. *Romans*. Atlanta: John Knox, 1985.

Barrett, C. K. *A Commentary on the Epistle to the Romans*. San Francisco: Harper & Row, 1958.

Barth, K. *Epistle to the Romans*. 6th ed. New York: Oxford University Press, 1968.

Black, M. *Romans*. Rev. ed. Grand Rapids: Eerdmans, 1981.

Bruce, F. F. *Romans*. Grand Rapids: Eerdmans, 1963.

*Cranfield, C. E. B. *A Critical and Exegetical Commentary on the Epistle to the Romans*. 2 vols. Edinburgh: Clark, 1975, 1979.

*_____. *Romans. A Shorter Commentary*. Grand Rapids: Eerdmans, 1985; Edinburgh: Clark.

Dodd, C. H. *The Epistle of Paul to the Romans* (1932). London: Collins, 1959.

Donfried, K. P., ed. *The Romans Debate*. Minneapolis: Augsburg, 1977.

Harrisville, R. A. *Romans.* Minneapolis: Augsburg, 1980.

*Käsemann, E. *Commentary on Romans.* Grand Rapids: Eerdmans, 1980.

Kuss, O. *Der Römerbrief. Übersetzt und erklärt.* 3 vols. Regensburg: F. Pustet, 1957, 1959, 1978.

Lagrange, M.—E. *Saint Paul: Epître aux Romains* (1916). Paris: Gabalda, 1950.

Maly, E. H. *Romans.* Wilmington: Michael Glazier, 1979.

Michel, O. *Der Brief an die Römer, übersetzt und erklärt.* 14th ed. Göttingen: Vandenhoeck & Ruprecht, 1978.

Robinson, J. A. T. *Wrestling with Romans.* Philadelphia: Westminster, 1979.

Sanday, W. and A. C. Headlam. *A Critical and Exegetical Commentary on the Epistle to the Romans.* Edinburgh: Clark, 1902.

Schlier, H. *Der Römerbrief. Kommentar.* Freiburg— Basel—Vienna: Herder, 1977.

Wilckens, U. *Der Brief an die Römer.* 3 vols. Cologne: Benziger, 1978, 1980, 1982; Neukirchen-Vluyn: Neukirchener.

50
1 Corinthians

Barrett, C. K. *A Commentary on the First Epistle to the Corinthians.* New York—Evanston, IL: Harper & Row, 1968.

Bruce, F. F. *Commentary on First and Second Corinthians.* Rev. ed. Grand Rapids: Eerdmans, 1981.

*Conzelmann, H. *1 Corinthians.* Philadelphia: Fortress, 1975.

*Murphy—O'Connor, J. *1 Corinthians.* Wilmington: Michael Glazier, 1979.

_____. *St. Paul's Corinth. Texts and Archaeology.* Wilmington: Michael Glazier, 1983.

Orr, W. F. and J. A. Walther, *1 Corinthians. A New Translation, Introduction with a Study of the Life of Paul, Notes, and Commentary.* Garden City, NY: Doubleday, 1976.

Robertson, A. and A. Plummer. *A Critical and Exegetical Commentary on the First Epistle of St. Paul to the Corinthians.* Edinburgh: Clark, 1914/1978.

Ruef, J. *Paul's First Letter to Corinth.* Philadelphia: Westminster, 1978.

51
2 Corinthians

Allo, E. B. *Saint Paul: Second Epître aux Corinthiens.* 2nd
    ed. Paris: Gabalda, 1956.

*Barrett, C. K. *A Commentary on the Second Epistle to the
    Corinthians.* New York: Harper & Row, 1974.

Bultmann, R. *The Second Letter to the Corinthians.*
    Minneapolis: Augsburg, 1985

Fallon, F. T. *2 Corinthians.* Wilmington: Michael Glazier,
    1980.

*Furnish, V. P. *II Corinthians.* Garden City, NY: Doubleday,
    1985.

Héring, J. *The Second Epistle of Saint Paul to the Corin-
    thians.* London: Epworth,1967.

52
Galatians

*Betz, H. D. *Galatians. A Commentary on Paul's Letter to the Churches in Galatia*. Philadelphia: Fortress, 1979.

*Bruce, F. F. *The Epistle to the Galatians. A Commentary on the Greek Text*. Grand Rapids: Eerdmans, 1982.

Burton, E. D. *A Critical and Exegetical Commentary on the Epistle to the Galatians* (1921). Edinburgh: Clark, 1977.

Lightfoot, J. B. *The Epistle of Paul to the Galatians* (1865). Grand Rapids: Zondervan, 1957.

Mussner, F. *Der Galaterbrief*. Freiburg—Vienna: Herder, 1974.

Osiek, C. *Galatians*. Wilmington: Michael Glazier, 1980.

53
Ephesians

Barth, M. *Ephesians: Introduction, Translation and Commentary.* 2 vols. Garden City, NY: Doubleday, 1974.

Gnilka, J. *Der Epheserbrief.* Freiburg—Vienna: Herder, 1971.

Goodspeed, E. J. *The Meaning of Ephesians.* Chicago: University of Chicago Press, 1933; London: Cambridge University Press.

Kirby, J. C. *Ephesians: Baptism and Pentecost. An Inquiry into the Structure and Purpose of the Epistle to the Ephesians.* Montreal: McGill University Press, 1968.

*Mitton, C. L. *Ephesians.* Greenwood, SC: Attic Press, 1976.

*Swain, L. *Ephesians.* Wilmington: Michael Glazier, 1980.

54
Philippians

Beare, F. W. *A Commentary on the Epistle to the Philippians.* 3rd ed. New York—San Francisco: Harper & Row, 1973.

Collange, J.—F. *The Epistle of Saint Paul to the Philippians.* London: Epworth, 1979.

Getty, M. A. *Philippians and Philemon.* Wilmington: Michael Glazier, 1980.

Gnilka, J. *Der Philipperbrief.* Freiburg—Vienna: Herder, 1968.

*Hawthorne, G. F. *Philippians.* Waco, TX: Word Books, 1983.

Houlden, J. L. *Paul's Letters from Prison. Phillippians, Colossians, Philemon, and Ephesians.* Baltimore: Penguin, 1970.

Lightfoot, J. B. *Saint Paul's Epistle to the Philippians.* Grand Rapids: Zondervan,1953.

Martin, R. P. *Philippians.* Greenwood, SC: Attic Press, 1976; London: Oliphants.

Vincent, M. R. *Epistles to the Philippians and Philemon.* Edinburgh: Clark, 1955.

55
Colossians

Bruce, F. F. *The Epistles to the Colossians, to Philemon, and to the Ephesians.* Grand Rapids: Eerdmans, 1984.

Gnilka, J. *Der Kolosserbrief.* Freiburg—Basel—Vienna: Herder, 1980.

*Lohse, E. *Colossians and Philemon.* Philadelphia: Fortress, 1971.

Martin, R. P. *Colossians: The Church's Lord and the Christian's Liberty.* Exeter, UK: Paternoster, 1972; Grand Rapids: Zondervan, 1973.

Moule, C. F. D. *The Epistles to the Colossians and to Philemon.* Cambridge, UK: Cambridge University Press, 1955.

O'Brien, P. T. *Colossians, Philemon.* Waco, TX: Word Books, 1982.

Rogers, P. *Colossians.* Wilmington: Michael Glazier, 1980.

*Schweizer, E. *The Letter to the Colossians. A Commentary.* Minneapolis: Augsburg, 1982; London: S.P.C.K.

56
1—2 Thessalonians

*Best, E. *A Commentary on the First and Second Epistles to the Thessalonians.* New York: Harper & Row, 1972.

Bruce, F. F. *1 & 2 Thessalonians.* Waco, TX: Word Books, 1982.

*Marshall, I. H. *1 and 2 Thessalonians.* Grand Rapids: Eerdmans, 1983; London: Marshall, Morgan & Scott.

Reese, J. *1 and 2 Thessalonians.* Wilmington: Michael Glazier, 1979.

Rigaux, B. *Saint Paul: Les Epîtres aux Thessaloniciens.* Paris: Gabalda, 1956.

Trilling, W. *Der zweite Brief an die Thessalonicher.* Zurich-Einsiedeln—Cologne: Benziger, 1980; Neukirchen—Vluyn: Neukirchener.

57
1—2 Timothy, Titus

*Dibelius, M. *The Pastoral Epistles.* Philadelphia: Fortress, 1972.

Dornier, P. *Les Epîtres pastorales.* Paris: Gabalda, 1969.

Hanson, A. T. *The Pastoral Epistles.* Grand Rapids: Eerdmans, 1982; London: Marshall, Morgan & Scott.

Houlden, J. L. *The Pastoral Epistles: I and II Timothy, Titus.* Harmordsworth, UK: Penguin, 1976.

Karris, R. J. *The Pastoral Epistles.* Wilmington: Michael Glazier, 1979.

Kelly, J. N. D. *A Commentary on the Pastoral Epistles (1964).* Grand Rapids: Baker, 1981.

Spicq, C. *Les Epîtres pastorales.* 2 vols. 2nd rev. ed. Paris: Gabalda, 1969.

58
Philemon

Getty, M. A. *Philippians and Philemon.* Wilmington: Michael Glazier, 1980.

Gnilka, J. *Der Philemonbrief.* Freiburg—Basel—Vienna: Herder, 1982.

*Lohse, E. *Colossians and Philemon.* Philadelphia: Fortress, 1971.

O'Brien, P. T. *Colossians, Philemon.* Waco, TX: Word, 1982.

59
Studies of Pauline Letters
(see §§ 48, 65-87)

Bassler, J. *Divine Impartiality. Paul and a Theological Axiom.* Chico: Scholars Press, 1982.

Brinsmead, B. H. *Galatians—Dialogical Response to Opponents.* Chico: Scholars Press, 1982.

Caragounis, C. *The Ephesian* Mysterion. *Meaning and Content.* Lund: C.W.K. Gleerup, 1977.

Collins, R. F. *Studies on the First Letter to the Thessalonians.* Leuven: Leuven University Press, 1984.

Crouch, J. F. *The Origin and Intention of the Colossian Haustafel.* Göttingen: Vandenhoeck & Ruprecht, 1972.

Klauck, H.—J. *Herrenmahl und hellenistischer Kult. Eine religionsgeschichtliche Untersuchung zum ersten Korintherbrief.* Münster: Aschendorff, 1982.

Lull, D. J. *The Spirit in Galatia. Paul's Interpretation of* Pneuma *as Divine Power.* Chico: Scholars Press, 1980.

Martin, R. P. *Carmen Christi. Philippians ii. 5-11 in Recent Interpretation and in the Setting of Early Christian Worship.* Rev. ed. Grand Rapids: Eerdmans, 1983.

Moxnes, H. *Theology in Conflict. Studies in Paul's Understanding of God in Romans.* Leiden: Brill, 1980.

Munck, J. *Christ and Israel. An Interpretation of Romans 9-11.* Philadelphia: Fortress, 1967.

Munro, W. *Authority in Paul and Peter. The Identification of a Pastoral Stratum in the Pauline Corpus and 1 Peter.* Cambridge, UK—London—New York: Cambridge University Press, 1983.

Prümm, K. *Diakonia Pneumatos. Der zweite Korintherbrief als Zugang zur apostolischen Botschaft. Auslegung und Theologie.* 3 vols. Freiburg—Vienna: Herder, 1960, 1962, 1967.

Stowers, S. K. *The Diatribe and Paul's Letter to the Romans.* Chico: Scholars Press, 1981.

Verner, D. C. *The Household of God. The Social World of the Pastoral Epistles.* Chico: Scholars Press, 1983.

Wagner, G. *Pauline Baptism and the Pagan Mysteries. The Problem of the Pauline Doctrine of Baptism in Romans VI. 1-11 in the Light of its Religio-Historical "Parallels."* Edinburgh—London: Oliver & Boyd, 1967.

Ziesler, J. A. *The Meaning of Righteousness in Paul. A Linguistic and Theological Inquiry.* New York—London: Cambridge University Press, 1972.

60
Hebrews

Braun, H. *An die Hebräer.* Tübingen: Mohr-Siebeck, 1984.

Bruce, F. F. *The Epistle to the Hebrews. The English Text with Introduction, Exposition and Notes.* Grand Rapids: Eerdmans, 1964.

Buchanan, G. W. *To the Hebrews: Translation, Comment, and Conclusions.* Garden City, NY: Doubleday, 1972.

Casey, J. *Hebrews.* Wilmington: Michael Glazier, 1980.

*Hagner, D. A. *Hebrews.* San Francisco: Harper & Row, 1983.

Héring, J. *The Epistle to the Hebrews.* London: Epworth, 1970.

Michel, O. *Der Brief an die Hebräer übersetzt und erklärt.* 12th rev. ed. Göttingen: Vandenhoeck & Ruprecht, 1966.

Moffatt, J. *A Critical and Exegetical Commentary on the Epistle to the Hebrews.* Edinburgh: Clark, 1924.

Montefiore, H. W. *The Epistle to the Hebrews.* New York: Harper & Row, 1964.

Smith, R. H. *Hebrews.* Minneapolis: Augsburg, 1984.

Spicq. C. *L'Epître aux Hébreux.* 2 vols. Paris: Gabalda, 1952-53.

—————— *L'Epître aux Hébreux.* Paris: Gabalda, 1977.

Vanhoye, A. *La Structure littéraire de l'Epître aux Hébreux.* Paris—Bruges: Desclée de Brouwer, 1963.

61
James, 1—2 Peter, Jude

*Bauckham, R. J. *Jude, 2 Peter*. Waco, TX: Word Books, 1983.

Beare, F. W. *The First Epistle of Peter. The Greek Text with Introduction and Notes*. 3rd rev. ed. Oxford: Blackwell, 1970.

Best, E. *1 Peter* (1971). Grand Rapids: Eerdmans, 1982.

Brox, N. *Der erste Petrusbrief*. Zurich—Einsiedeln—Cologne: Benziger, 1979; Neukirchen-Vluyn: Neukirchener.

Davids, P. D. *The Epistle of James. A Commentary on the Greek Text*. Grand Rapids: Eerdmans, 1982.

_____ *James*. San Francisco: Harper & Row, 1983.

*Dibelius, M. *James. A Commentary on the Epistle of James*. Philadelphia: Fortress, 1976.

Elliott, J. H. and R. A. Martin. *James. I-II Peter/Jude*. Minneapolis: Augsburg, 1982.

Goppelt, L. *Der Erste Petrusbrief.* Göttingen: Vandenhoeck & Ruprecht, 1978.

Kelly, J. N. D. *A Commentary on the Epistles of Peter and of Jude.* New York—Evanston, IL: Harper & Row, 1970.

Kugelman, R. *James & Jude.* Wilmington: Michael Glazier, 1980.

Laws, S. *A Commentary on the Epistle of James.* San Francisco: Harper & Row, 1980.

Mitton, C. L. *The Epistle of James.* Grand Rapids: Eerdmans, 1966.

Mussner, F. *Der Jakobusbrief.* Freiburg: Herder, 1964.

Reicke, B. *The Epistles of James, Peter, and Jude.* New York: Doubleday, 1964.

Ropes, J. H. *A Critical and Exegetical Commentary on the Epistle of St. James* (1916). Edinburgh: Clark, 1978.

Schelkle, K. H. *Die Petrusbriefe, der Judasbrief.* Freiburg: Herder, 1961.

Selwyn, E. G. *The First Epistle of St. Peter. The Greek Text with Introduction, Notes, and Essays* (1947). Grand Rapids: Baker, 1981.

*Senior, D. *1 & 2 Peter.* Wilmington: Michael Glazier, 1980.

Spicq, C. *Les Epîtres de saint Pierre.* Paris: Gabalda, 1966.

62
1—3 John
(see § 42)

*Brown, R. E. *The Epistles of John. Translated with Introduction, Notes, and Commentary.* Garden City, NY: Doubleday, 1982.

Bultmann, R. *The Johannine Epistles.* Philadelphia: Fortress, 1973.

Dodd, C. H. *The Johannine Epistles.* New York: Harper, 1946.

Grayston, K. *The Johannine Epistles.* Grand Rapids: Eerdmans, 1984; London: Marshall, Morgan & Scott.

Houlden, J. L. *A Commentary on the Johannine Epistles.* New York: Harper & Row, 1974.

Marshall, I. H. *The Epistles of John.* Grand Rapids: Eerdmans, 1978.

Perkins, P. *The Johannine Epistles.* Wilmington: Michael Glazier, 1979.

Schnackenburg, R. *Die Johannesbriefe.* 4th ed. Freiburg: Herder, 1970.

Smalley, S. S. *1, 2, 3 John.* Waco, TX: Word Books, 1983.

63
Revelation

Beasley-Murray, G. *The Book of Revelation* (1974). Grand Rapids: Eerdmans, 1981.

Caird, G. B. *A Commentary on the Revelation of St. John the Divine.* New York—Evanston: Harper & Row, 1966.

Charles, R. H. *A Critical and Exegetical Commentary on the Revelation of St. John.* 2 vols. Edinburgh: Clark, 1920.

Harrington, W. J. *Understanding the Apocalypse.* Washington, DC—Cleveland: Corpus, 1969.

Kraft, H. *Die Offenbarung des Johannes.* Tübingen: Mohr, 1974.

Minear, P. S. *I Saw a New Earth. An Introduction to the Visions of the Apocalypse.* Washington, DC—Cleveland: Corpus, 1969.

Mounce, R. H. *The Book of Revelation.* Grand Rapids: Eerdmans, 1977.

Sweet, J. P. M. *Revelation.* Philadelphia: Westminster, 1979.

*Yarbro Collins, A. *The Apocalypse.* Wilmington: Michael Glazier, 1979.

64
Studies of Non-Pauline Letters

Balch, D. L. *Let Wives Be Submissive. The Domestic Code in I Peter.* Chico: Scholars Press, 1981.

Bogart, J. *Orthodox and Heretical Perfectionism in the Johannine Community as Evident in the First Epistle of John.* Missoula: Scholars, 1977.

Corsini, E. *The Apocalypse. The Perennial Revelation of Jesus Christ.* Wilmington: Michael Glazier, 1983.

Dalton, W. J. *Christ's Proclamation to the Spirits. A Study of 1 Peter 3:18—4:6.* Rome: Biblical Institute Press, 1965.

D'Angelo, M. R. *Moses in the Letter to the Hebrews.* Missoula: Scholars Press, 1979.

Demarest, B. *A History of Interpretation of Hebrews 7, 1-10 from the Reformation to the Present.* Tübingen: Mohr-Siebeck, 1976.

Elliott, J. H. *The Elect and the Holy. An Exegetical Examination of 1 Peter 2:4-10 and the Phrase* basileion hierateuma. Leiden: Brill, 1966.

*————————. *A Home for the Homeless. A Sociological Exegesis of 1 Peter, Its Situation and Strategy.* Philadelphia: Fortress, 1981.

Fornberg, T. *An Early Church in a Pluralistic Society. A Study of 2 Peter.* Lund: C.W.K. Gleerup, 1977.

Horton, F. L. *The Melchizedek Tradition. A Critical Examination of the Sources to the Fifth Century A.D. and in the Epistle to the Hebrews.* Cambridge, UK—London—New York: Cambridge University Press, 1976.

Hughes, G. *Hebrews and Hermeneutics. The Epistle to the Hebrews as a New Testament Example of Biblical Interpretation.* New York—London: Cambridge University Press, 1979.

*Käsemann, E. *The Wandering People of God. An Investigation of the Letter to the Hebrews.* Minneapolis: Augsburg, 1984.

Lambrecht, J., ed. *L'Apocalypse johannique et l'Apocalyptique dans le Nouveau Testament.* Gembloux: Duculot, 1980; Leuven: Leuven University Press.

Malatesta, E. *Interiority and Covenant. A Study of* einai en *and* menein en *in the First Letter of John.* Rome: Biblical Institute Press, 1978.

Peterson, D. *Hebrews and Perfection. An Examination of the Concept of Perfection in the "Epistle to the Hebrews."* Cambridge, UK—London—New York: Cambridge University Press, 1982.

*Schüssler Fiorenza, E. *The Book of Revelation: Justice and Judgment.* Philadelphia: Fortress, 1985.

Segovia, F. F. *Love Relationships in the Johannine Tradition. Agapē/Agapan in I John and the Fourth Gospel.* Chico: Scholars Press, 1982.

Thompson, J. W. *The Beginnings of Christian Philosophy: The Epistle to the Hebrews.* Washington, DC: Catholic Biblical Association of America, 1982.

Vanhoye, A. *Situation du Christ. Hébreux 1—2.* Paris: Cerf, 1969.

Williamson, R. *Philo and the Epistle to the Hebrews.* Leiden: Brill, 1970.

Yarbro Collins, A. *The Combat Myth in the Book of Revelation.* Missoula: Scholars Press, 1976.

*_____ *Crisis and Catharsis: The Power of the Apocalypse.* Philadelphia: Westminster, 1984.

V. New Testament Theology

65
New Testament Theology

Boers, H. *What Is New Testament Theology? The Rise of Criticism and the Problem of a Theology of the New Testament.* Philadelphia: Fortress, 1979.

Bornkamm, G. *Early Christian Experience.* New York: Harper & Row, 1970.

Childs, B. S. *Biblical Theology in Crisis.* Philadelphia: Westminster, 1970.

Hasel, G. F. *New Testament Theology. Basic Issues in the Current Debate.* Grand Rapids: Eerdmans, 1978.

Jeremias, J. *The Central Message of the New Testament.* New York: Scribner's, 1965.

Käsemann, E. *Essays on New Testament Themes.* Naperville, IL: Allenson, 1964.

_____. *New Testament Questions of Today.* Philadelphia: Fortress, 1969.

_____. "The Problem of a New Testament Theology." *New Testament Studies* 19 (1973) 235-45.

Malet, A. *The Thought of Rudolf Bultmann.* Garden City, NY: Doubleday, 1970.

*Morgan, R. *The Nature of New Testament Theology. The Contribution of William Wrede and Adolf Schlatter.* London: SCM, 1973.

Perrin, N. *The Promise of Bultmann.* Philadelphia—New York: Lippencott, 1969.

Smart, J. D. *The Past, Present, and Future of Biblical Theology.* Philadelphia: Fortress, 1979.

66
Theologies of the New Testament

*Bultmann, R. *Theology of the New Testament.* 2 vols. New York: Scribner's, 1955.

Conzelmann, H. *An Outline of the Theology of the New Testament.* New York—Evanston, IL: Harper & Row, 1969.

Cullmann, O. *Salvation in History.* New York—Evanston, IL: Harper & Row, 1967.

Goppelt, L. *Theology of the New Testament.* 2 vols. Grand Rapids: Eerdmans, 1981, 1983.

Guthrie, D. *New Testament Theology.* Downers Grove, IL—Leicester, UK: Inter-Varsity, 1981.

Kümmel, W. G. *The Theology of the New Testament According to Its Major Witnesses: Jesus—Paul—John.* Nashville—New York: Abingdon, 1973.

Ladd, G. E. *A Theology of the New Testament.* Grand Rapids: Eerdmans, 1974.

Schelkle, K. H. *Theology of the New Testament.* 4 vols.
    Collegeville, MN: Liturgical Press, 1971, 1973, 1976,
    1978.

Stauffer, E. *New Testament Theology.* London: SCM, 1955;
    New York: Macmillan.

67
Anthropology

Brandenburger, E. *Fleisch und Geist. Paulus und die dualist-ische Weisheit.* Neukirchen-Vluyn: Neukirchener, 1968.

Byrne, B. *'Sons of God' — 'Seed of Abraham.' A Study in the Idea of the Sonship of God of all Christians in Paul against the Jewish Background.* Rome: Biblical Institute Press, 1979.

Cerfaux, L. *The Christian in the Theology of St. Paul.* New York: Herder & Herder, 1967.

Gundry, R. H. *Soma in Biblical Theology. With Emphasis on Pauline Anthropology.* Cambridge, UK—London —New York: Cambridge University Press, 1976.

Jewett, R. *Paul's Anthropological Terms. A Study of Their Use in Conflict Settings.* Leiden: Brill, 1971.

*Murphy—O'Connor, J. *Becoming Human Together. The Pastoral Anthropology of St. Paul.* Wilmington: Michael Glazier, 1982.

Robinson, J. A. T. *The Body. A Study in Pauline Theology.*
2nd ed. Philadelphia: Westminster, 1977.

Sand, A. *Der Begriff "Fleisch" in den paulinischen Haupt-
briefen.* Regensburg: F. Pustet, 1967.

Scroggs, R. *The Last Adam. A Study in Pauline Anthropology.* Philadelphia: Fortress, 1966.

68
Baptism

Aland, K. *Did the Early Church Baptize Infants?* Philadelphia: Fortress, 1963.

Beasley-Murray, G. R. *Baptism in the New Testament.* New York: St. Martin's Press, 1962.

Cullmann, O. *Baptism in the New Testament* (1950). Philadelphia: Westminster, 1978.

Dunn, J. D. G. *Baptism in the Holy Spirit. A Re-examination of the New Testament Teaching on the Gift of the Holy Spirit in Relation to Pentecostalism Today.* Naperville, IL: Allenson, 1970.

Jeremias, J. *The Origins of Infant Baptism. A further study in reply to Kurt Aland.* Naperville, IL: Allenson, 1963.

*Schnackenburg, R. *Baptism in the Thought of St. Paul. A Study in Pauline Theology.* New York: Herder & Herder, 1964.

69
Christology
(see § 34)

Bible et christologie. Commission Biblique Pontificale. Paris: Cerf, 1984.

Bousset, W. *Kyrios Christos. A History of the Belief in Christ from the Beginnings of Christianity to Irenaeus.* Nashville: Abingdon, 1970.

Brown, R. E. "'Who Do Men Say That I Am?' —Modern Scholarship on Gospel Christology." *Horizons* 1 (1974) 35-50.

Cerfaux, L. *Christ in the Theology of St. Paul.* New York: Herder & Herder, 1959.

*Cullmann, O. *The Christology of the New Testament.* Philadelphia: Westminster, 1959.

*Dunn, J. D. G. *Christology in the Making. A New Testament Inquiry Into the Origins of the Doctrine of the Incarnation.* Philadelphia: Westminster, 1980.

Dupont, J., ed. *Jésus aux origines de la christologie.* Gembloux: Duculot, 1975; Leuven: Leuven University Press.

*Fitzmyer, J. A. *A Christological Catechism. New Testament Answers.* New York—Ramsey, NJ: Paulist, 1982.

Fuller, R. H. *The Foundations of New Testament Christology.* New York: Scribner's, 1965.

_____ and P. Perkins. *Who Is This Christ? Gospel Christology and Contemporary Faith.* Philadelphia: Fortress, 1983.

Hahn, F. *The Titles of Jesus in Christology. Their History in Early Christianity.* New York—Cleveland: World, 1969.

Hengel, M. *The Son of God. The Origin of Christology and the History of Jewish-Hellenistic Religion.* Philadelphia: Fortress, 1976.

Hooker, M. D. "Christology and Methodology." *New Testament Studies* 17 (1971) 480-87.

Hurtado, L. W. "New Testament Christology: A Critique of Bousset's Influence." *Theological Studies* 40 (1979) 306-17.

*Moule, C. F. D. *The Origin of Christology.* Cambridge, UK—London—New York: Cambridge University Press, 1977.

Neyrey, J. H. *Christ is Community: The Christologies of the New Testament.* Wilmington: Michael Glazier, 1985.

Sabourin, L. *Christology: Basic Texts in Focus.* New York: Alba House, 1984.

Schillebeeckx, E. *Jesus. An Experiment in Christology.* New York: Seabury, 1979.

_____. *Christ. The Experience of Jesus as Lord.* New York: Seabury, 1980.

Schweizer, E. *Jesus.* Richmond, VA—London: John Knox, 1971.

Vawter, B. *This Man Jesus. An Essay Toward a New Testament Christology.* Garden City, NY: Doubleday, 1973.

70
Christological Motifs

Becker, J. *Messianic Expectation in the Old Testament.* Philadelphia: Fortress, 1980.

Borsch, F. H. *The Son of Man in Myth and History.* Philadelphia: Westminster, 1967.

Brown, R. E. *Jesus God and Man. Modern Biblical Reflections.* Milwaukee: Bruce, 1967.

Burger, C. *Jesus als Davidsohn. Ein traditionsgeschichtliche Untersuchung.* Göttingen: Vandenhoeck & Ruprecht, 1970.

Casey, M. *Son of Man. The interpretation and influence of Daniel 7.* London: S.P.C.K., 1979.

Christ, F. *Jesus Sophia. Die Sophia-Christologie bei den Synoptikern.* Zurich: Zwingli, 1970.

Craddock, F. B. *The Pre-existence of Christ in the New Testament.* Nashville—New York: Abingdon, 1968.

Dahl, N. *The Crucified Messiah and other essays.* Minneapolis: Augsburg, 1974.

Daly, R. J. "The Soteriological Significance of the Sacrifice of Isaac." *Catholic Biblical Quarterly* 39 (1977) 45-75.

Davies, P. R. and B. D. Chilton. "The Aqedah: A Revised Tradition History." *Catholic Biblical Quarterly* 40 (1978) 514-46.

de Jonge, M. "The use of the word 'anointed' in the time of Jesus." *Novum Testamentum* 8 (1966) 132-48.

Duling, D. C. "Solomon, Exorcism, and the Son of David." *Harvard Theological Review* 68 (1975) 235-52.

Feuillet, A. *Le Christ Sagesse de Dieu d'après les epîtres pauliniennes.* Paris: Gabalda, 1966.

Fitzmyer, J. A. "The Ascension of Christ and Pentecost." *TheologicalStudies* 45 (1984) 409-40.

Hamerton-Kelly, R. G. *Pre-Existence, Wisdom, and the Son of Man. A Study of the Idea of Pre-Existence in the New Testament.* New York: Cambridge University Press, 1973.

Hengel, M. *The Atonement. The Origins of the Doctrine in the New Testament.* Philadelphia: Fortress, 1981.

Higgins, A. J. B. *The Son of Man in the Teaching of Jesus.* New York—Cambridge, UK—London: Cambridge University Press, 1980.

Holladay, C. R. Theios Aner *in Hellenistic Judaism: A Critique of the Use of This Category in New Testament Christology.* Missoula: Scholars Press, 1977.

Hooker, M. D. *Jesus and the Servant. The Influence of the Servant Concept of Deutero-Isaiah in the New Testament.* London: S.P.C.K., 1959.

_____. *The Son of Man in Mark. A Study of the background of the term "Son of Man" and its use in St. Mark's Gospel.* London: S.P.C.K., 1967.

Käsemann, E. *Jesus Means Freedom.* Philadelphia: Fortress, 1970.

Kearns, R. *Vorfragen zur Christologie.* 3 vols. Tübingen: Mohr-Siebeck, 1978, 1980, 1982.

Kim, S. *"The 'Son of Man'" as the Son of God.* Tübingen: Mohr-Siebeck, 1983; Grand Rapids: Eerdmans, 1985.

Kingsbury, J. D. *Jesus Christ in Matthew, Mark, and Luke.* Philadelphia: Fortress, 1981.

Kramer, W. *Christ, Lord, Son of God.* Naperville, IL: Allenson, 1966.

Lindars, B. *Jesus Son of Man. A Fresh Examination of the Son of Man Sayings in the Gospels in the Light of Recent Research.* London: S.P.C.K., 1983.

Matera, F. J. *The Kingship of Jesus. Composition and Theology in Mark 15.* Chico: Scholars Press, 1982.

Neusner, J. *Messiah in Context. Israel's History and Destiny in Formative Judaism.* Philadelphia: Fortress, 1984.

Perrin, N. *A Modern Pilgrimage in New Testament Christology.* Philadelphia: Fortress, 1974.

Sanders, J. T. *The New Testament Christological Hymns. Their Historical Religious Background.* New York—London: Cambridge University Press, 1971.

Smith, M. "Prolegomena to a Discussion of Aretalogies, Divine Men, the Gospels and Jesus." *Journal of Biblical Literature* 90 (1971) 174-99.

Stanley, D. M. *Christ's Resurrection in Pauline Soteriology.* Rome: Biblical Institute Press, 1961.

Stanton, G. N. *Jesus of Nazareth in New Testament Preaching.* New York: Cambridge University Press, 1975.

Tannehill, R. C. *Dying and Rising with Christ. A Study in Pauline Theology.* Berlin: Töpelmann, 1967.

Tiede, D. L. *The Charismatic Figure as Miracle Worker.* Missoula: Society of Biblical Literature, 1972.

Tödt, H. E. *The Son of Man in the Synoptic Tradition.* Philadelphia: Westminster, 1965.

Vermes, G. "The Present State of the 'Son of Man' Debate." *Journal of Jewish Studies* 29 (1978) 123-34.

Walker, W. O. "The Son of Man: Some Recent Developments." *Catholic Biblical Quarterly* 45 (1983) 584-607.

Wikenhauser, A. *Pauline Mysticism. Christ in the Mystical Teaching of St. Paul.* New York: Herder & Herder, 1960.

Wrede, W. *The Messianic Secret*. Greenwood, SC: Attic Press, 1971; London: Clarke.

Young, F. M. *Sacrifice and the Death of Christ*. London: S.P.C.K., 1975.

Zimmerli, W. and J. Jeremias. *The Servant of God*. Naperville, IL: Allenson, 1965.

71
Church
(see § 79)

Banks, R. *Paul's Idea of Community. The Early House Churches in their Historical Setting.* Grand Rapids: Eerdmans, 1980.

Barth, M. *The People of God.* Sheffield, UK: JSOT Press, 1983.

*Brown, R. E. *The Churches the Apostles Left Behind.* New York—Ramsey, NJ: Paulist, 1984.

_____. "The Unity and Diversity in New Testament Ecclesiology." *Novum Testamentum* 6 (1963) 298-308.

Cerfaux, L. *The Church in the Theology of St. Paul.* New York: Herder & Herder, 1959.

Cody, A. "The Foundation of the Church: Biblical Criticism for Ecumenical Discussion." *Theological Studies* 34 (1973) 3-18.

Dunn, J. D. G. *Unity and Diversity in the New Testament. An Inquiry Into the Character of Earliest Christianity.* Philadelphia: Westminster, 1977.

Hahn, F. *Mission in the New Testament.* Naperville, IL: Allenson, 1965.

Hainz, J. *Koinonia. "Kirche" als Gemeinschaft bei Paulus.* Regensburg: F. Pustet, 1982.

*Harrington, D. J. *God's People in Christ. New Testament Perspectives on the Church and Judaism.* Philadelphia: Fortress, 1979.

——————. *The Light of All Nations. Essays on the Church in New Testament Research.* Wilmington: Michael Glazier, 1982.

Hilgert, E. *The Ship and Related Symbols in the New Testament.* Assen: van Gorcum, 1962.

Käsemann, E. "Unity and Diversity in New Testament Ecclesiology." *Novum Testamentum* 6 (1963) 290-97.

Klauck, H.—J. *Hausgemeinde und Hauskirche im frühen Christentum.* Stuttgart: Katholisches Bibelwerk, 1981.

Knox, J. *The Early Church and the Coming Great Church.* Nashville: Abingdon, 1955.

Lohfink, G. *Jesus and Community. The Social Dimension of Christian Faith.* Philadelphia: Fortress, 1984; New York—Ramsey, NJ: Paulist.

McDermott, J. M. "The Biblical Doctrine of *KOINŌNIA*." *Biblische Zeitschrift* 19 (1975) 64-77, 219-33.

McKelvey, R. J. *The New Temple. The Church in the New Testament.* New York: Oxford University Press, 1969.

Minear, P. S. *Images of the Church in the New Testament.* Philadelphia: Westminster, 1960.

Nickle, K. F. *The Collection. A Study in Paul's Strategy.* Naperville, IL: Allenson, 1966.

Sampley, J. P. *Pauline Partnership in Christ. Christian Community and Commitment in Light of Roman Law.* Philadelphia: Fortress, 1980.

Schnackenburg, R. *The Church in the New Testament.* New York: Herder & Herder, 1965.

Senior, D. and C. Stuhlmueller. *The Biblical Foundations for Mission.* Maryknoll, NY: Orbis Books, 1983.

von Allmen, D. *La famille de Dieu. La symbolique familiale dans le paulinisme.* Fribourg: Editions Universitaires, 1981; Göttingen: Vandenhoeck & Ruprecht.

72
Eschatology
(see §§ 35, 93)

Aune, D. E. *The Cultic Setting of Realized Eschatology in Early Christianity*. Leiden: Brill, 1972.

Beker, J. C. *Paul's Apocalyptic Gospel. The Coming Triumph of God*. Philadelphia: Fortress, 1982.

Bultmann, R. *History and Eschatology*. Edinburgh: University Press, 1957; New York: Harper & Row.

Carmignac, J. *Le Mirage de l'Eschatologie. Royauté, Règne et Royaume de Dieu ... sans Eschatologie*. Paris: Letouzey & Ané, 1979.

Davies, W. D. and D. Daube, eds. *The Background of the New Testament and its Eschatology*. New York— Cambridge, UK: Cambridge University Press, 1964.

Lincoln, A. T. *Paradise Now and Not Yet. Studies in the role of the heavenly dimension in Paul's thought with special reference to his eschatology*. Cambridge, U.K. —London—New York: Cambridge University Press, 1981.

Minear, P. S. *New Testament Apocalyptic*. Nashville: Abingdon, 1981.

Moore, A. L. *The Parousia in the New Testament*. Leiden: Brill, 1966.

*Schnackenburg, R. *God's Rule and Kingdom*. New York: Herder & Herder, 1963.

Shires, H. M. *The Eschatology of Paul in the Light of Modern Scholarship*. Philadelphia: Westminster, 1966.

73
Ethics

Birch, B. C. and L. L. Rasmussen. *Bible and Ethics in the Christian Life.* Minneapolis: Augsburg, 1976.

Corriveau, R. *The Liturgy of Life. A Study of the Ethical Thought of St. Paul in His Letters to the Early Christian Communities.* Brussels—Paris: Desclée de Brouwer, 1970; Montreal: Bellarmin.

Curran, C. E. and R. A. McCormick, eds. *Readings in Moral Theology No. 4: The Use of Scripture in Moral Theology.* New York—Ramsey, NJ: Paulist, 1984.

Daly, R. J. et al. *Christian Biblical Ethics. From Biblical Revelation to Contemporary Christian Praxis: Method and Content.* New York—Ramsey, NJ: Paulist, 1984.

Deidun, T. J. *New Covenant Morality in Paul.* Rome: Biblical Institute Press, 1981.

Fuller, R. H., ed. *Essays on the Love Commandment.* Philadelphia: Fortress, 1978.

Furnish, V. P. *The Moral Teaching of Paul. Selected Issues.* Rev. ed. Nashville: Abingdon, 1985.

_____. *Theology and Ethics in Paul.* Nashville—New York: Abingdon, 1968.

Gerhardsson, B. *The Ethos of the Bible.* Philadelphia: Fortress, 1981.

Hiers, R. H. *Jesus and Ethics. Four Interpretations.* Philadelphia: Westminster, 1968.

Houlden, J. L. *Ethics and the New Testament.* Baltimore: Penguin, 1973.

Longenecker, R. N. *New Testament Social Ethics for Today.* Grand Rapids: Eerdmans, 1984.

Mohrlang, R. *Matthew and Paul. A Comparison of Ethical Perspectives.* Cambridge, UK—London—New York: Cambridge University Press, 1984.

Mott, S. C. *Biblical Ethics and Social Change.* New York—Oxford: Oxford University Press, 1982.

Ogletree, T. W. *The Use of the Bible in Christian Ethics. A Constructive Essay.* Philadelphia: Fortress, 1983.

Osborn, E. *Ethical Patterns in Early Christian Thought.* Cambridge, UK—London—New York—Melbourne: Cambridge University Press, 1976.

Perkins, P. *Love Commands in the New Testament.* New York—Ramsey, NJ: Paulist, 1982.

Pierce, C. A. *Conscience in the New Testament.* Chicago: Allenson, 1955.

Piper, J. *'Love your enemies.' Jesus' Love Command in the Synoptic Gospels and in Early Christian Paraenesis. A History of the Tradition and Interpretation of Its Uses.* New York—Cambridge, UK—London: Cambridge University Press, 1979.

Richardson, P. *Paul's Ethic of Freedom.* Philadelphia: Westminster, 1979.

Sanders, J. T. *Ethics in the New Testament. Change and Development.* Philadelphia: Fortress, 1975.

Schnackenburg, R. *The Moral Teaching of the New Testament.* New York: Herder & Herder, 1965.

Schrage, W. *Ethik des Neuen Testaments.* Göttingen: Vandenhoeck & Ruprecht, 1982.

Spicq, *Agape in the New Testament.* 3 vols. St. Louis—London: B. Herder, 1963, 1965, 1966.

—————. *Théologie Morale du Nouveau Testament.* Paris: Gabalda, 1965.

*Spohn, W. C. *What Are They Saying About Scripture and Ethics?* New York—Ramsey, NJ: Paulist, 1984.

Verhey, A. *The Great Reversal. Ethics and the New Testament.* Grand Rapids: Eerdmans, 1984.

Wendland, H. D. *Ethik des Neuen Testaments. Eine Einführung.* Göttingen: Vandenhoeck & Ruprecht, 1970.

White, R. E. O. *Biblical Ethics.* Atlanta: John Knox, 1979.

74
Eucharist

Aune, D. E. "The Presence of God in the Community: The Eucharist in its Early Christian Cultic Context." *Scottish Journal of Theology* 29 (1976) 451-59.

Feeley-Harnik, G. *The Lord's Table. Eucharist and Passover in Early Christianity.* Philadelphia: University of Pennsylvania Press, 1981.

Jeremias, J. *The Eucharistic Words of Jesus.* New York: Scribner's, 1966.

Kilmartin, E. J. *The Eucharist in the Primitive Church.* Englewood Cliffs, NJ: Prentice-Hall, 1965.

Kilpatrick, G. D. *The Eucharist in Bible and Liturgy.* Cambridge, UK—London—New York: Cambridge University Press, 1983.

Léon-Dufour, X. *Le partage du pain eucharistique selon le Nouveau Testament.* Paris: Seuil, 1982.

Lietzmann, H. *Mass and the Lord's Supper. A Study in the History of Liturgy.* Leiden: Brill, 1979.

Marshall, I. H. *Last Supper and Lord's Supper.* Exeter, UK: Paternoster, 1980; Grand Rapids: Eerdmans, 1981.

Schweitzer, A. *The Problem of the Lord's Supper According to the Scholarly Research of the Nineteenth Century and the Historical Accounts. Volume 1: The Lord's Supper in Relationship to the Life of Jesus and the History of the Early Church.* Macon, GA: Mercer University Press, 1982.

75
Holy Spirit

Bruner, F. D. *A Theology of the Holy Spirit. The Pente-costal Experience and the New Testament Witness.* Grand Rapids: Eerdmans, 1970.

*Dunn, J. D. G. *Jesus and the Spirit. A Study of the Religious and Charismatic Experience of Jesus and the First Christians as Reflected in the New Testament.* Phila-delphia: Westminster, 1975; London: SCM.

Isaacs, M. E. *The Concept of Spirit. A Study of Pneuma in Hellenistic Judaism and its Bearing on the New Testa-ment.* London: Heythrop College, 1976.

Lampe, G. W. H. *God as Spirit.* Oxford: Clarendon Press, 1977.

Montague, G. T. *The Holy Spirit: Growth of a Biblical Tradition.* New York—Paramus, NJ—Toronto: Paulist, 1976.

Moule, C. F. D. *The Holy Spirit.* Oxford: Mowbray, 1978; Grand Rapids: Eerdmans, 1979.

Schweizer, E. *The Holy Spirit.* Philadelphia: Fortress, 1980.

76
Jews and Christians
(see § 39)

Baum, G. *The Jews and the Gospel. A Re-examination of the New Testament.* Westminster, MD: Newman, 1961.

Davies. A. T., ed. *Antisemitism and the Foundations of Christianity.* New York—Ramsey, NJ—Toronto: Paulist, 1979.

Davies, W. D. "Paul and the People of Israel." *New Testament Studies* 24 (1977) 4-39.

*Gager, J. G. *The Origins of Anti-Semitism. Attitudes Toward Judaism in Pagan and Christian Antiquity.* New York: Oxford University Press, 1983.

Hagner, D. A. *The Jewish Reclamation of Jesus. An Analysis and Critique of Modern Jewish Study of Jesus.* Grand Rapids: Zondervan, 1984.

Klein, C. *Anti-Judaism in Christian Theology.* Philadelphia: Fortress, 1978.

Koenig, J. *Jews and Christians in Dialogue: New Testament Foundations.* Philadelphia: Westminster, 1979.

Munck, J. *Paul and the Salvation of Mankind.* London: SCM, 1959; Richmond, VA: John Knox, 1960.

Mussner, F. *Tractate on the Jews. The Significance of Judaism for Christian Faith.* Philadelphia: Fortress, 1984; London: S.P.C.K.

Räisänen, H. *Paul and the Law.* Tübingen: Mohr-Siebeck, 1983.

Refoulé, F. *". . .et ainsi tout Israël sera sauvé." Romains 11, 25-32.* Paris: Cerf, 1984.

Richardson, P. *Israel in the Apostolic Church.* New York: Cambridge University Press, 1970.

Sanders, E. P. *Paul, the Law, and the Jewish People.* Philadelphia: Fortress, 1983.

*Sandmel, S. *Anti-Semitism in the New Testament?* Philadelphia: Fortress, 1978.

_____. *The First Christian Century in Judaism and Christianity: Certainties and Uncertainties.* New York: Oxford University Press, 1969.

_____. *A Jewish Understanding of the New Testament.* Cincinnati: Hebrew Union College Press, 1957.

_____. *Judaism and Christian Beginnings.* New York: Oxford University Press, 1978.

_____. *We Jews and Jesus.* New York: Oxford University Press, 1965.

Sevenster, *The Roots of Pagan Anti-Semitism in the Ancient World.* Leiden: Brill, 1975.

Sloyan, G. *Is Christ the End of the Law?* Philadelphia: Westminster, 1978.

*Stendahl, K. *Paul Among Jews and Gentiles and Other Essays.* Philadelphia: Fortress, 1976.

Thoma, C. *A Christian Theology of Judaism.* New York— Ramsey, NJ: Paulist, 1980.

Williamson, C. M. *Has God Rejected His People? Anti-Judaism in the Christian Church.* Nashville: Abingdon, 1982.

77
Marriage and Divorce

*Fitzmyer, J. A. "The Matthean Divorce Texts and Some Palestinian Evidence." *Theological Studies* 37 (1976) 197-226.

Isaksson, A. *Marriage and Ministry in the New Temple. A Study with Special Reference to Mt. 19, 3-12 and 1 Cor. 11.3-16.* Lund: C.W.K. Gleerup, 1965.

Sampley, J. P. *'And the Two Shall Become One Flesh.' A Study of Traditions in Ephesians 5:21-33.* New York—London—Cambridge University Press, 1971.

Vawter, B. "Divorce and the New Testament." *Catholic Biblical Quarterly* 39 (1977) 528-42.

78
Mary

Bearsley, P. J. "Mary the Perfect Disciple: A Paradigm for Mariology." *Theological Studies* 41 (1980) 461-504.

*Brown, R. E., et al. *Mary in the New Testament. A Collaborative Assessment by Protestant and Roman Catholic Scholars.* Philadelphia: Fortress, 1978; New York—Ramsey, NJ—Toronto: Paulist.

Feuillet, A. *Jesus and His Mother According to the Lucan Infancy Narratives, and According to St. John. The Role of the Virgin Mary in Salvation History and the Place of Women in the Church.* Still River, MA: St. Bede's Publications, 1984.

McHugh, J. *The Mother of Jesus in the New Testament.* Garden City, NY: Doubleday, 1975.

Tambasco, A. J. *What Are They Saying About Mary?* New York—Ramsey, NJ: Paulist, 1984.

79
Ministry
(see § 71)

*Brown, R. E. *Priest and Bishop. Biblical Reflections.* Paramus, NJ—Toronto: Paulist, 1970.

_____ "*Episkopē* and *Episkopos*: The New Testament Evidence." *Theological Studies* 41 (1980) 322-38.

*_____ et al. *Peter in the New Testament. A Collaborative Effort by Protestant and Roman Catholic Scholars.* New York—Toronto: Paulist, 1973; Minneapolis: Augsburg.

Cullmann, O. *Peter: Disciple, Apostle, Martyr. A Historical and Theological Study.* 2nd rev. ed. Philadelphia: Westminster, 1962.

Delorme, J., ed. *Le ministère et les ministères selon le Nouveau Testament. Dossier exégètique et réflexion théologique.* Paris: Seuil, 1974.

Elliott, J. H. "Ministry and Church Order in the New Testament: A Traditio-Historical Analysis (1 Pt 5, 1-5) and plls." *Catholic Biblical Quarterly* 32 (1970) 367-91.

Ferguson, E. "Laying On of Hands: Its Significance in Ordination." *Journal of Theological Studies* 26 (1975) 1-12.

Freyne, S. *The Twelve: Disciples and Apostles. A Study in the theology of the first three Gospels.* London—Sydney: Sheed & Ward, 1968.

Funk, A. *Status und Rollen in den Paulusbriefen. Eine inhaltsanalytische Untersuchung zur Religionssoziologie.* Innsbruck—Vienna—Munich: Tyrolia Verlag, 1981.

Hainz, J., ed. *Kirche im Werden. Studien zum Thema Amt und Gemeinde im Neuen Testament.* Munich—Paderborn—Vienna: Schöningh, 1976.

Harvey, A. E. "Elders." *Journal of Theological Studies* 25 (1974) 318-32.

Holmberg, B. *Paul and Power. The Structure of Authority in the Primitive Church as Reflected in the Pauline Epistles.* Philadelphia: Fortress, 1980.

Kertelge, K., ed. *Das kirchliche Amt im Neuen Testament.* Darmstadt: Wissenschaftliche Buchgesellschaft, 1977.

Koenig, J. *Charismata: God's Gifts for God's People.* Philadelphia: Westminster, 1978.

Lemaire, A. *Ministry in the Church.* London: S.P.C.K., 1977.

_____. "The Ministries in the New Testament. Recent Research." *Biblical Theology Bulletin* 3 (1973) 133-66.

Murphy-O'Connor, J. *Paul on Preaching.* New York: Sheed & Ward, 1964.

Ollrog, W.-H. *Paulus und seine Miterbeiter. Untersuchungen zu Theorie und Praxis der paulinischen Mission.* Neukirchen-Vlyun: Neukirchener, 1979.

Perkins, P. *Ministering in the Pauline Churches.* New York—Ramsey, NJ: Paulist, 1982.

Rengstorf, K. H. *Apostolate and Ministry. The New Testament Doctrine of the Office of the Ministry.* St. Louis—London: Concordia, 1969.

Schmithals, W. *The Office of Apostle in the Early Church.* Nashville—New York: Abingdon, 1969.

Schütz, J. H. *Paul and the Anatomy of Apostolic Authority.* New York: Cambridge University Press, 1975.

Schweizer, E. *Church Order in the New Testament.* Naperville, IL: Allenson, 1961.

Spicq, C. "La place ou le rôle des jeunes dans certaines communautés neotestamentaires." *Revue Biblique* 76 (1969) 508-27.

Stanley, D. M. "The New Testament Basis for the Concept of Collegiality." *Theological Studies* 25 (1964) 197-216.

Vanhoye, A. *Prêtres anciens, prêtre nouveau selon le Nouveau Testament.* Paris: Seuil, 1980.

von Campenhausen, H. *Ecclesiastical Authority and Spiritual Power in the Church of the First Three Centuries.* Stanford, CA: Stanford University Press, 1969.

80
Old Testament in the
New Testament

Archer, G. L. and G. Chirichigno. *Old Testament Quotations in the New Testament*. Chicago: Moody, 1983.

Black, M. "The Christological Use of the Old Testament in the New Testament." *New Testament Studies* 18 (1971) 1-14.

Bratcher, R. G. *Old Testament Quotations in the New Testament*. 2nd rev. ed. London—New York—Stuttgart: United Bible Societies, 1984.

Chilton, B. D. *A Galilean Rabbi and His Bible. Jesus' Use of the Interpreted Scripture of His Time*. Wilmington: Michael Glazier, 1984.

Dodd, C. H. *According to the Scriptures. The Sub-Structure of New Testament Theology*. London: Collins, 1965.

Doeve, J. W. *Jewish Hermeneutics in the Synoptic Gospels and Acts*. Assen: van Gorcum, 1954.

Fitzmyer, J. A. "The Use of Explicit Old Testament Quotations in Qumran Literature and in the New Testament." *New Testament Studies* 7 (1961) 297-333.

France, R. T. *Jesus and the Old Testament. His Application of Old Testament Passages to Himself and His Mission* (1971). Grand Rapids: Baker, 1982.

Goppelt, L. *Typos. The Typological Interpretation of the Old Testament in the New.* Grand Rapids: Eerdmans, 1982.

Hanson, A. T. *The Living Utterances of God. The New Testament Exegesis of the Old.* London: Darton, Longman and Todd, 1983.

_____. *The New Testament Interpretation of Scripture.* London: S.P.C.K., 1980.

Hay, D. M. *God at the Right Hand. Psalm 110 in Early Christianity.* Nashville—New York: Abingdon, 1973.

*Lindars, B. *New Testament Apologetic. The Doctrinal Significance of Old Testament Quotations.* Philadelphia: Westminster, 1961.

_____ and P. Borgen. "The Place of the Old Testament in the Formation of New Testament Theology. Prolegomena and Response." *New Testament Studies* 23 (1976) 59-75.

Longenecker, R. N. *Biblical Exegesis in the Apostolic Period.* Grand Rapids: Eerdmans, 1975.

Patte, D. *Early Jewish Hermeneutic in Palestine.* Missoula: Scholars Press, 1975.

Shires, H. M. *Finding the Old Testament in the New.* Philadelphia: Westminster, 1974.

81
Politics

Bammel, E. and C. F. D. Moule, eds. *Jesus and the Politics of His Day*. Cambridge, UK—London—New York: Cambridge University Press, 1984.

Barr, J. "The Bible as a Political Document." *Bulletin of the John Rylands University Library of Manchester* 62 (1980) 268-89.

Brandon, S. G. F. *Jesus and the Zealots. A Study of the Political Factor in Primitive Christianity*. New York: Scribner's, 1967; Manchester: University of Manchester Press.

Cullmann, O. *Jesus and the Revolutionaries*. New York—London: Harper & Row, 1970.

_____. *The State in the New Testament*. New York: Scribner's, 1966.

Daly, R. J. "The New Testament: Pacifism and Non-Violence." *American Ecclesiastical Review* 168 (1974) 544-62.

Furnish, V. P. "War and Peace in the New Testament." *Interpretation* 38 (1984) 363-79.

Harnack, A. *Militia Christi: The Christian Religion and the Military in the First Three Centuries.* Philadelphia: Fortress, 1981.

*Hengel, M. *Christ and Power.* Philadelphia: Fortress, 1977.

*_____. *Victory over Violence. Jesus and the Revolutionists.* Philadelphia: Fortress, 1973.

82
Powers

Caird, G. B. *Principalities and Powers. A Study in Pauline Theology.* Oxford: Oxford University Press, 1956.

Carr, W. *Angels and Principalities, The background, meaning and development of the Pauline phrase* kai archai kai hai exousiai. Cambridge, UK—London—New York: Cambridge University Press, 1981.

Russell, J. B. *The Devil: Perceptions of Evil from Antiquity to Primitive Christianity.* Ithaca, NY—London: Cornell University Press, 1977.

_____. *Satan: The Early Christian Tradition.* Ithaca, NY—London: Cornell University Press, 1981.

*Schlier, H. *Principalities and Powers in the New Testament.* New York: Herder & Herder, 1961.

Wink, W. *Naming the Powers. The Language of Power in the New Testament.* 3 vols. Philadelphia: Fortress, 1984-

83
Prophecy

*Aune, D. E. *Prophecy in Early Christianity and the Ancient Mediterranean World.* Grand Rapids: Eerdmans, 1983.

Hill, D. *New Testament Prophecy.* Atlanta: John Knox, 1979; London: Marshall, Morgan & Scott.

Panagopoulos, J., ed. *Prophetic Vocation in the New Testament and Today.* Leiden: Brill, 1977.

84
Rich and Poor

*Hengel, M. *Property and Riches in the Early Church. Aspects of a Social History of Early Christianity*. Philadelphia: Fortress, 1974.

Johnson, L. T. *Sharing Possessions. Mandate and Symbol of Faith*. Philadelphia: Fortress, 1981.

Mealand, D. L. *Poverty and Expectation in the Gospels*. London: S.P.C.K., 1980.

Stegemann, W. *The Gospel and the Poor*. Philadelphia: Fortress, 1984.

85
Woman

Gerstenberger, E. S. and W. Schrage. *Woman and Man*. Nashville: Abingdon, 1981.

Hamerton—Kelly, R. *God the Father. Theology and Patriarchy in the Teaching of Jesus*. Philadelphia: Fortress, 1979.

Kraemer, R. S. "Women in the Religions of the Greco-Roman World." *Religious Studies Review* 9 (1983) 127-39.

Meeks, W. A. "The Image of the Androgyne: Some Uses of a Symbol in Earliest Christianity." *History of Religions* 13 (1974) 165-208.

Schelkle, K. H. *The Spirit and the Bride: Woman in the Bible*. Collegeville, MN: Liturgical Press, 1979.

*Schüssler Fiorenza, E. *In Memory of Her. A Feminist Theological Reconstruction of Christian Origins*. New York: Crossroad, 1983.

Witherington, B. *Women in the Ministry of Jesus. A Study of Jesus' Attitudes to Women and Their Roles as Reflected in His Earthly Life.* Cambridge, UK—London —New York: Cambridge University Press, 1984.

86
Worship

Charlesworth, J. H. "A Prolegomenon to a New Study of the Jewish Background of the Hymns and Prayers in the New Testament." *Journal of Jewish Studies* 33 (1982) 265-85.

Cullmann, O. *Early Christian Worship* (1953). Philadelphia: Westminster, 1978.

Delling, G. *Worship in the New Testament*. Philadelphia: Westminster, 1962.

Hahn, F. *The Worship of the Early Church*. Philadelphia: Fortress, 1973.

*Martin, R. P. *Worship in the Early Church*. Grand Rapids: Eerdmans, 1975.

Stanley, D. M. *Boasting in the Lord. The Phenomenon of Prayer in Saint Paul*. New York—Toronto: Paulist, 1973.

Wiles, G. P. *Paul's Intercessory Prayers. The Significance of the Intercessory Prayer Passages in the Letters of St. Paul*. New York: Cambridge University Press, 1974.

87
Various Themes

Bailey, L. *Biblical Perspectives on Death.* Philadelphia: Fortress, 1979.

Cullmann, O. *Immortality of the Soul, or Resurrection of the Dead? The Witness of the New Testament.* New York: Macmillan, 1958.

Daly, R. J. *The Origins of the Christian Doctrine of Sacrifice.* Philadelphia: Fortress, 1978.

Davies, W. D. *The Gospel and the Land, Early Christianity and Jewish Territorial Doctrine.* Berkeley, CA—London: University of California Press, 1974.

Gerstenberger, E. S. and W. Schrage. *Suffering.* Nashville: Abingdon, 1980.

Gibbs, J. G. *Creation and Redemption: A Study in Pauline Theology.* Leiden: Brill, 1971.

Gunneweg, A. H. J. and W. Schmithals, *Achievement.* Nashville: Abingdon, 1981.

Hermisson, H.-J. and E. Lohse. *Faith*. Nashville: Abingdon, 1981.

Herrmann, S. *Time and History*. Nashville: Abingdon, 1981.

Kaiser, O. and E. Lohse. *Death and Life*. Nashville: Abingdon, 1981.

Lyonnet, S. and L. Sabourin. *Sin, Redemption, and Sacrifice. A Biblical and Patristic Study*. Rome: Biblical Institute Press, 1970.

McDonald, J. I. H. *Kerygma and Didache. The articulation and structure of the earliest Christian message*. Cambridge, UK—New York: Cambridge University Press, 1980.

Morrice, W. G. *Joy in the New Testament*. Exeter, UK: Paternoster, 1984.

Otto, E. and T. Schramm. *Festival and Joy*. Nashville: Abingdon, 1980.

Reumann, J. *"Righteousness" in the New Testament. "Justification" in the United States Luterthan-Roman Catholic Dialogue*. Philadelphia: Fortress, 1982; New York—Ramsey, NJ: Paulist.

Scroggs, R. *The New Testament and Homosexuality. Contextual Background for Contemporary Debate*. Philadelphia: Fortress, 1983.

Seybold, K. and U. B. Müller. *Sickness and Healing*. Nashville: Abingdon, 1981.

Simundson, D. J. *Faith Under Fire. Biblical Interpretations of Suffering*. Minneapolis: Augsburg, 1980.

Steck, O. H. *World and Environment*. Nashville: Abingdon, 1980.

Trites, A. A. *The New Testament Concept of Witness*. Cambridge, UK—London—New York: Cambridge University Press, 1977.

Wimmer, J. F. *Fasting in the New Testament. A Study in Biblical Theology*. New York—Ramsey, NJ—Toronto: Paulist, 1982.

VI. World of the
New Testament

88
Anthologies

Austin, M. M., ed. *The Hellenistic World from Alexander to the Roman Conquest. A Selection of Ancient Sources in Translation.* Cambridge, UK—London—New York: Cambridge University Press, 1981.

Barrett, C. K., ed. *The New Testament Background: Selected Documents.* New York: Harper & Row, 1961.

Cartlidge, D. R. and D. L. Dungan, eds. *Documents for the Study of the Gospels.* Philadelphia: Fortress, 1980.

Chisholm, K. and J. Ferguson, eds. *Rome: The Augustan Age. A Source Book.* Oxford—New York: Oxford University Press, 1981.

Ferguson, J., ed. *Greek and Roman Religion. A Source Book.* Park Ridge, NJ: Noyes Press, 1980.

Grant, F. C., ed. *Ancient Roman Religion.* Indianapolis—New York: Bobbs-Merrill, Liberal Arts Press, 1980.

_____, ed. *Hellenistic Religions. The Age of Syncretism*. Indianapolis—New York: Bobbs-Merrill, Liberal Arts Press, 1953.

*Kee, H. C, ed. *The New Testament in Context. Sources and Documents*. Englewood Cliffs, NJ: Prentice-Hall, 1984.

89
Greco-Roman World

Badian, E. *Publicans and Sinners. Private Enterprise in the Service of the Roman Republic. With a Critical Bibliography*. Rev. ed. Ithaca, NY—London: Cornell University Press, 1983.

Balsdon, J. P. V. D. *Romans and Aliens*. Chapel Hill, NC: University of North Carolina Press, 1979.

Bruce, F. F. "The New Testament and Classical Studies." *New Testament Studies* 22 (1976) 229-42.

Christ, K. *The Romans. An Introduction to Their History and Civilisation*. Berkeley, CA—Los Angeles: University of California Press, 1984.

Deissmann, A. *Light From the Ancient East. The New Testament Illustrated by Recently Discovered Texts of the Greco-Roman World* (1927). Grand Rapids: Baker, 1965.

Fraser, P. W. *Ptolemaic Alexandria*. 3 vols. Oxford: Clarendon Press, 1985.

Grant, F. C. *Roman Hellenism and the New Testament.* New York: Scribner's, 1962.

Grant, M. *From Alexander to Cleopatra. The Hellenistic World.* New York: Scribner's, 1982.

Grese, W. "The Hermetica and New Testament Research." *Biblical Research* 28 (1983) 37-54.

*Gruen, E. S. *The Hellenistic World and the Coming of Rome.* 2 vols. Berkeley, CA—Los Angeles—London: University of California Press, 1984.

Haase, W., ed. *Aufstieg und Niedergang der römischen Welt. Geschichte und Kultur Roms im Spiegel der neueren Forschung.* Berlin—New York: de Gruyter, 1979-

Hammond, N. G. L., ed. *Atlas of the Greek and Roman World in Antiquity.* Park Ridge, NJ: Noyes Press, 1981.

Horsley, G. H. R., ed. *New Documents Illustrating Early Christianity. A Review of the Greek Inscriptions and Papyri.* North Ryde, Australia: Ancient History Documentary Research Centre, 1981-

Jones, A. H. M. *The Cities of the Eastern Roman Provinces.* Oxford: Clarendon Press, 1937.

Lewis, N. *Life in Egypt Under Roman Rule.* New York: Clarendon Press, Oxford University Press, 1983.

MacMullen, R. *Paganism in the Roman Empire.* New Haven—London: Yale University Press, 1981.

_____. *Roman Social Relations. 50 B.C. to A.D. 284*. New Haven—London: Yale University Press, 1974.

Magie, D. *Roman Rule in Asia Minor, to the End of the Third Century after Christ*. 2 vols. Princeton, NJ: Princeton University Press, 1950.

May, H. G. et al., *Oxford Bible Atlas*. 3rd rev. ed. New York—Toronto: Oxford University Press, 1984.

Millar, F. *The Emperor in the Roman World (31 BC-AD 337)*. Ithaca, NY: Cornell University Press, 1977.

*Momigliano, A. *Alien Wisdom. The Limits of Hellenization*. Cambridge, UK—London—New York—Melbourne: Cambridge University Press, 1976.

Nilsson, M. *A History of Greek Religion* (1925). New York: Norton, 1964.

Nock, A. D. *Conversion. The Old and the New in Religion from Alexander the Great to Augustine of Hippo* (1933). Oxford: Oxford University Press, 1961.

_____. *Essays on Religion and the Ancient World*. 2 vols. Cambridge, MA: Harvard University Press, 1972; Oxford: Clarendon Press.

Reitzenstein, R. *Hellenistic Mystery-Religions. Their Basic Ideas and Significance*. Pittsburgh: Pickwick Press, 1978.

Rostovtzeff, M. *The Social and Economic History of the Hellenistic World*. 3 vols. 2nd ed. Oxford: Clarendon Press, 1952.

_____. *The Social and Economic History of the Roman Empire*. 2 vols. 2nd ed. by P. M. Fraser. Oxford: Clarendon Press, 1957.

Sherwin-White, A. N. *Roman Society and the Roman Law in the New Testament, The Sarum Lectures 1960-1961*. New York—London: Oxford University Press, 1963.

Stern, M., ed. *Greek and Latin Authors on Jews and Judaism*. 2 vols. Jerusalem: Israel Academy of Sciences and Humanities, 1976.

Tarn, W. W. *Hellenistic Civilisation*. 3rd ed. Cleveland— New York: World, 1961.

Teixidor, J. *The Pagan God. Popular Religion in the Greco-Roman Near East*. Princeton, NJ: Princeton University Press, 1977.

van Unnik, W. C. "Words come to Life. The Work for the 'Corpus Hellenisticum Novi Testamenti.'" *Novum Testamentum* 13 (1971) 199-216.

Widengren, G., ed. *Der Mandäismus*. Darmstadt: Wissenschaftliche Buchgesellschaft, 1982.

90
Archaeology

Avi-Yonah, M. and E. Stern, eds. *Encyclopedia of Archaeological Excavations in the Holy Land.* 4 vols. Englewood Cliffs, NJ: Prentice-Hall, 1975; Jerusalem: Israel Exploration Society.

Blaiklock, E. M. *The Archaeology of the New Testament.* Rev. ed. Nashville: Nelson, 1984.

_____ and R. K. Harrison, eds. *The New International Dictionary of Biblical Archaeology.* Grand Rapids: Zondervan, 1983.

Finegan, J. *The Archaeology of the New Testament. The Life of Jesus and the Beginning of the Early Church.* Princeton, NJ: Princeton University Press, 1970.

_____. *The Archaeology of the New Testament. The Mediterranean World of the Early Christian Apostles.* Boulder, CO: Westview Press, 1981; London: Croom Helm.

Finley, M. I., ed. *Atlas of Classical Archaeology.* New York: McGraw-Hill, 1977.

Goodenough, E. R. *Jewish Symbols in the Greco-Roman Period.* 13 vols. New York: Bollingen, 1953-65.

Klaiber, W. "Archäologie und Neues Testament." *Zeitschrift für Neutestamentliche Wissenschaft* 72 (1981) 195-215.

Kopp, C. *The Holy Places of the Gospels.* New York: Herder & Herder, 1963.

*Meyers, E. M. and J. F. Strange. *Archaeology, the Rabbis, and Early Christianity: The Social and Historical Setting of Palestinian Judaism and Christianity.* Nashville: Abingdon, 1981.

Murphy-O'Connor, J. *The Holy Land. An Archaeological Guide from Earliest Times to 1700.* Oxford—New York: Oxford University Press, 1980.

Niccacci, A. "L'ambiente del Nuovo Testamento e della chiesa primitiva alla luce degli scavi dello Studium Biblicum Franciscanum (Gerusalemme)." *Antonianum* 58 (1983) 6-47.

Snyder, G. F., *Ante Pacem. Archaeological Evidence of Church Life before Constantine.* Macon. GA: Mercer University Press, 1985.

Stillwell, R., ed. *The Princeton Encyclopedia of Classical Sites.* Princeton, NJ: Princeton University Press, 1976.

Wilkinson, J. *Jerusalem as Jesus knew it. Archaeology as Evidence.* New York—London: Thames and Hudson, 1978.

*Yamauchi, E. M. *The Archaeology of New Testament Cities in Western Asia Minor.* Grand Rapids: Baker, 1980.

91
Jewish History

Abel, F.-M. *Histoire de la Palestine depuis la conquête d'Alexandre jusqu'a l'invasion arabe.* 2 vols. Paris: Gabalda, 1952.

Avi-Yonah, M. and Z. Baras, eds. *The Herodian Period.* New Brunswick, NJ: Rutgers University Press, 1975.

Crown, A. D. *A Bibliography of the Samaritans.* Metuchen, NJ—London: Scarecrow Press, 1984.

Davies, W. D. and L. Finkelstein, eds. *The Cambridge History of Judaism.* 4 vols. Cambridge, UK—New York: Cambridge University Press, 1984-

Freyne, S. *Galilee from Alexander the Great to Hadrian, 323 B.C.E. to 135 C.E. A Study of Second Temple Judaism.* Wilmington: Michael Glazier, 1980.

Goodman, M. *State and Society in Roman Galilee, A.D. 132-212.* Totowa, NJ: Rowman & Allanheld, 1983.

Hengel, M. *Jews, Greeks and Barbarians. Aspects of the Hellenization of Judaism in the pre-Christian Period.* Philadelphia: Fortress, 1980; London: SCM.

*_____. *Judaism and Hellenism. Studies in Their Encounter in Palestine during the Early Hellenistic Period.* 2 vols. Philadelphia: Fortress, 1974.

_____. *Die Zeloten. Untersuchungen zur jüdischen Freiheitsbewegung in der Zeit von Herodes I. bis 70 n. Chr.* Rev. ed. Leiden—Cologne: Brill, 1976.

Hoehner, H. *Herod Antipas.* New York—London: Cambridge University Press, 1972.

Horsley, R. A. "Popular Messianic Movements around the Time of Jesus." *Catholic Biblical Quarterly* 46 (1984) 471-95.

Jeremias, J. *Jerusalem in the Time of Jesus. An Investigation into Economic and Social Conditions during the New Testament Period.* Philadelphia: Fortress, 1969.

Mor, M. and U. Rappaport, eds. *Bibliography of Works on Jewish History in the Hellenistic and Roman Periods, 1976-1980.* Jerusalem: Zalman Shazar Center, Historical Society of Israel, 1982.

Rivkin, E. *A Hidden Revolution. The Pharisees' Search for the Kingdom Within.* Nashville: Abingdon, 1978.

Safrai, S. and M. Stern, eds. *The Jewish People in the First Century. Historical Geography, Political History, Social Cultural and Religious Life and Institutions.* 2 vols. Philadelphia: Fortress, 1974, 1976.

Schalit, A., ed. *The Hellenistic Age. Political History of Jewish Palestine from 332 B.C.E. to 67 B.C.E.* Jerusalem: Masada, 1972.

*Schürer, E. *The History of the Jewish People in the Age of Jesus Christ (175 B.C.-A.D. 135)*. Rev. ed., by G. Vermes and F. Millar. 2 vols. Edinburgh: Clark, 1973, 1979.

Smallwood, E. M. *The Jews under Roman Rule. From Pompey to Diocletian*. Leiden: Brill, 1976.

Smith, M. "Zealots and Sicarii, Their Origins and Relation." *Harvard Theological Review* 64 (1971) 1-19.

Stone, M. E. *Scriptures, Sects and Visions. A Profile of Judaism from Ezra to the Jewish Revolts*. Philadelphia: Fortress, 1980.

Tcherikover, V. *Hellenistic Civilization and the Jews*. Philadelphia: Jewish Publication Society of America, 1959.

92
Second Temple Jewish Writings

Charles, R. H., ed. *The Apocypha and Pseudepigrapha of the Old Testament.* 2 vols. Oxford: Clarendon Press, 1913.

*Charlesworth, J. H., ed. *The Old Testament Pseudepigrapha.* 2 vols. Garden City, NJ: Doubleday, 1983, 1985.

_____. *The Pseudepigrapha and Modern Research with a Supplement.* Chico: Scholars, 1981.

Collins, J. J. *Between Athens and Jerusalem. Jewish Identity in the Hellenistic Diaspora.* New York: Crossroad, 1983.

Delling, G., ed. *Bibliographie zur jüdisch-hellenistischen und intertestamentarischen Literatur: 1900-1970.* 2nd rev. ed. Berlin: Akademie-Verlag, 1975.

Denis, A.-M. *Introduction aux pseudepigraphes grecs d'Ancien Testament.* Leiden: Brill, 1970.

Kümmel, W. G., ed. *Jüdische Schriften aus hellenistisch-römischer Zeit.* 6 vols. Gütersloh: Mohn, 1973-

McNamara, M. *Intertestamental Literature*. Wilmington: Michael Glazier, 1983.

——————. *Palestinian Judaism and the New Testament*. Wilmington: Michael Glazier, 1983.

Nickelsburg, G. W. E. *Jewish Literature Between the Bible and the Mishnah. A Historical and Literary Introduction*. Philadelphia: Fortress, 1981.

—————— and M. E. Stone. *Faith and Piety in Early Judaism. Texts and Documents*. Philadelphia: Fortress, 1983.

*Stone, M. E., ed. *Jewish Writings of the Second Temple Period. Apocrypha, Pseudepigrapha, Qumran Sectarian Writings, Philo, Josephus*. Philadelphia: Fortress, 1984.

93
Jewish Apocalypticism
(see §§ 35, 72)

*Collins, J. J. *The Apocalyptic Imagination. An Introduction to the Jewish Matrix of Christianity.* New York: Crossroad, 1984.

_____, ed. *Apocalypse. The Morphology of a Genre.* Semeia 14. Missoula: Scholars, 1979.

Funk, R. W., ed. *Apocalypticism.* Journal for Theology and the Church, vol. 6. New York: Herder & Herder, 1969.

Hanson, P. D. *The Dawn of Apocalyptic.* 2nd ed. Philadelphia: Fortress, 1979.

_____, ed. *Visionaries and their Apocalypses.* Philadelphia: Fortress, 1983; London: S.P.C.K.

Hellholm, D., ed. *Apocalypticism in the Mediterranean World and the Near East. Proceedings of the International Colloquium on Apocalypticism, Uppsala, August 12-17, 1979.* Tübingen: Mohr-Siebeck, 1983.

Koch, K. *The Rediscovery of Apocalyptic.* London: SCM, 1972.

_____ and J. M. Schmidt, eds. *Apokalyptik*. Darmstadt: Wissenschaftliche Buchgesellschaft, 1982.

Mowinckel, S. *He That Cometh*. New York: Abingdon, 1956.

Nickelsburg, G. W. E. *Resurrection, Immortality, and Eternal Life in Intertestamental Judaism*. Cambridge, MA: Harvard University Press, 1972.

Rowland, C. *The Open Heaven. A Study of Apocalyptic in Judaism and Early Christianity*. New York: Crossroad, 1982.

Russell, D. S. *The Method and Message of Jewish Apocalyptic, 200 BC-AD 100*. Philadelphia: Westminster, 1964.

Schmithals, W. *The Apocalyptic Movement. Introduction and Interpretation*. Nashville—New York: Abingdon, 1975.

94
Dead Sea Scrolls

Black, M. *The Scrolls and Christian Origins. Studies in the Jewish Background of the New Testament.* New York: Scribner's, 1961.

Braun, H. *Qumran und das Neue Testament.* 2 vols. Tübingen: Mohr-Siebeck, 1966.

Cross, F. M. *The Ancient Library of Qumran and Modern Biblical Studies.* Garden City, NY: Doubleday, 1958.

_____ and S. Talmon, eds. *Qumran and the History of the Biblical Text.* Cambridge, MA—London: Harvard University Press, 1975.

Davies, P. R. *Qumran.* Grand Rapids: Eerdmans, 1983.

de Vaux, R. *Archaeology and the Dead Sea Scrolls.* New York: Oxford University Press, 1973.

Driver, G. R. *The Judaean Scrolls. The Problem and a Solution.* Oxford: Blackwell, 1965.

Dupont-Sommer, A. *The Essene Writings from Qumran* (1961). Gloucester/Magnolia, MA: Peter Smith, 1973.

*Fitzmyer, J. A. *The Dead Sea Scrolls. Major Publications and Tools for Study.* Rev. ed. Missoula: Scholars Press, 1977.

_____. "The Dead Sea Scrolls and the New Testament after thirty years." *Theology Digest* 29 (1981) 351-67.

Grözinger, K. E., ed. *Qumran.* Darmstadt: Wissenschaftliche Buchgesellschaft, 1981.

Jongeling, B. *A Classified Bibliography of the Finds in the Desert of Judah 1958-1969.* Leiden: Brill, 1971.

La Sor, W. S. *Bibliography of the Dead Sea Scrolls 1948-1957.* Pasadena, CA: Fuller Theological Seminary, 1958.

Milik, J. T. *Ten Years of Discovery in the Wilderness of Judaea.* Naperville, IL: Allenson, 1959.

Murphy-O'Connor, J. "The Essenes and their History." *Revue Biblique* 81 (1974) 215-44.

Ringgren, H. *The Faith of Qumran. Theology of the Dead Sea Scrolls.* Philadelphia: Fortress, 1963.

Stendahl, K., ed. *The Scrolls and the New Testament.* New York: Harper and Brothers, 1957.

*Vermes, G. *The Dead Sea Scrolls. Qumran in Perspective.* Cleveland: Collins & World, 1978.

_____. The Dead Sea Scrolls in English. Harmonds-
worth, UK—Baltimore: Penguin Books, 1962.

_____. "The Impact of the Dead Sea Scrolls on the
Study of the New Testament." *Journal of Jewish
Studies* 27 (1976) 107-16.

Yadin, Y . *The Temple Scroll. The Hidden Law of the Dead
Sea Sect*. New York: Random House, 1985.

Yizhar, M. *Bibliography of Hebrew Publications on the
Dead Sea Scrolls 1948-1964*. Cambridge, MA: Harvard University Press, 1967.

95
Josephus and Philo

*Colson, F. H. and G. H. Whitaker. *Philo, with an English Translation.* 12 vols. Cambridge, MA: Harvard University Press, 1929-62; London: Heinemann.

*Feldman, L. H. *Josephus and Modern Scholarship (1937-1980).* Berlin—New York: de Gruyter, 1984.

Goodenough, E. R. *An Introduction to Philo Judaeus.* 2nd ed. New Haven: Yale University Press, 1962; London: Oxford University Press.

Radice, R. *Filone di Alessandria. Bibliografia, 1937-1982.* Naples: Bibliopolis, 1983.

*Rajak, T. *Josephus. The Historian and His Society.* Philadelphia: Fortress, 1984.

Rengstorf, K. H., ed. *A Complete Concordance to Flavius Josephus.* 4 vols. Leiden: Brill, 1973-83.

*Sandmel, S. *Philo of Alexandria. An Introduction.* New York: Oxford University Press, 1979.

Schreckenberg, H. *Bibliographie zu Flavius Josephus; Supplementband mit Gesamtregister.* Leiden: Brill, 1968, 1979.

*Thackeray, H. St. J. et al., *Josephus, with an English Translation.* 9 vols. Cambridge, MA: Harvard University Press, 1926-65; London: Heinemann.

Wolfson, H. A. *Philo.* 2 vols. Cambridge, MA: Harvard University Press, 1947.

96
Rabbinic Writings

Alexander, P. S. "Rabbinic Judaism and the New Testament." *Zeitschrift für Neutestamentliche Wissenschaft* 74 (1983) 237-46.

Bokser, B. M. "Recent Developments in the Study of Judaism 70-200 C.E." *Second Century* 3 (1983) 1-68.

*Danby, H. *The Mishnah, Translated from the Hebrew with Introduction and Brief Explanatory Notes* (1933). Oxford: Clarendon Press, 1954.

Daube, D. *The New Testament and Rabbinic Judaism*. London: Athlone, 1956; New York: John de Graff.

Epstein, I., ed. *The Babylonian Talmud*. 35 vols. London: Soncino, 1935-52.

Freedman, H. and M. Simon, eds. *Midrash Rabbah*. 10 vols. London—Bournemouth: Soncino, 1951.

McNamara, M. "Some Recent Writings on Rabbinic Literature and the Targums." *Milltown Studies* 9 (1982) 59-101.

Moore, G. F. *Judaism in the First Centuries of the Christian Era. The Age of the Tannaim* (1927, 1930). 2 vols. New York: Schocken, 1971.

Neusner, J. *Judaism in Society. The Evidence of the Yerushalmi. Toward the Natural History of a Religion.* Chicago—London: University of Chicago Press, 1983.

_____. Judaism: The Evidence of the Mishnah. Chicago—London: University of Chicago Press, 1981.

_____. "'Judaism' after Moore. A Programmatic Statement." *Journal of Jewish Studies* 31 (1980) 141-56.

_____. "Map Without Territory. Mishnah's System of Sacrifice and Sanctuary." *History of Religions* 19 (1979) 103-27.

_____. "Methodology in Talmudic History." *Biblical Theology Bulletin* 14 (1984) 99-109.

_____. *Midrash in Context. Exegesis in Formative Judaism. The Foundations of Judaism: Method, Teleology, Doctrine. Part One: Method.* Philadelphia: Fortress, 1983.

_____. *The Talmud of Babylonia. An American Translation.* 26 vols. Chico: Scholars Press, 1984—

_____. *The Talmud of the Land of Israel.* 35 vols. Chicago—London: University of Chicago Press, 1982—

*_____. *The Tosefta Translated from the Hebrew.* 6 vols. New York: Ktav, 1977-81.

_____, ed. *The Study of Ancient Judaism.* 2 vols. New York: Ktav, 1981.

Strack, H. L. *Introduction to the Talmud and Midrash.* Philadelphia: Jewish Publication Society of America, 1931.

_____ and P. Billerbeck, *Kommentar zum Neuen Testament aus Talmud und Midrasch.* 6 vols. Munich: Beck, 1922-61.

Urbach, E. E. *The Sages. Their Concepts and Beliefs.* 2 vols. Jerusalem: Magnes, 1975.

Vermes, G. "Jewish Literature and New Testament Exegesis: Reflections on Methodology." *Journal of Jewish Studies* 33 (1982) 361-76.

_____. "Jewish Studies and New Testament Interpretation." *Journal of Jewish Studies* 31 (1980) 1-17.

Weiss Halivni, D. "Contemporary Methods of the Study of the Talmud." *Journal of Jewish Studies* 30 (1979) 192-201.

97
Targums

Bowker, J. *The Targums and Rabbinic Literature. An Introduction to Jewish Interpretations of Scripture.* New York: Cambridge University Press, 1969.

Churgin, P. *Targum Jonathan to the Prophets* (1927). New York: Ktav, 1983; Baltimore: Baltimore Hebrew College.

Clarke, E. G. et al. *Targum Pseudo-Jonathan of the Pentateuch: Text and Concordance.* Hoboken, NJ: Ktav, 1984.

Díez-Macho, A. ed. *Neofiti 1: Targum Palestinense, Ms de la Biblioteca Vaticana.* 5 vols. Madrid: Consejo Superior de Investigaciones Cientificas, 1968-78.

Etheridge, J. W. *The Targums of Onkelos and Jonathan Ben Uzziel on the Pentateuch with the Fragments of the Jerusalem Targum from the Chaldee* (1862, 1865). New York: Ktav, 1968.

Forestell, J. T. *Targumic Traditions and the New Testament. An Annotated Bibliography with a New Testament Index.* Chico: Scholars Press, 1979.

Grossfeld, B. *A Bibliography of Targum Literature.* 2 vols. New York: Ktav, 1972, 1977.

Kaufman, S. A. "On Methodology in the Study of the Targums and Chronology." *Journal for the Study of the New Testament* 23 (1985) 117-24.

Klein, M. L. *The Fragment-Targums of the Pentateuch According to their Extant Sources.* 2 vols. Rome: Biblical Institute Press, 1980.

*Le Déaut, R. *The Message of the New Testament and the Aramaic Bible (Targum).* Rome: Biblical Institute Press, 1982.

_____. *Targum du Pentateuque. Traduction des deux recensions palestiniennes complètes avec introduction, paralleles, notes et index.* 5 vols. Paris: Cerf, 1978-81.

_____. "Targumic Literature and New Testament Interpretation." *Biblical Theology Bulletin* 4 (1974) 243-89.

McNamara, M. "Half a Century of Targum Study." *Irish Biblical Studies* 1 (1979) 157-68.

_____. *The New Testament and the Palestinian Targum to the Pentateuch.* Rome: Biblical Institute Press, 1966.

_____. *Targum and Testament. Aramaic Paraphrases of the Hebrew Bible: A Light on the New Testament.* Shannon: Irish University Press, 1972; Grand Rapids: Eerdmans.

Nickels, P. *Targum and New Testament. A Bibliography together with a New Testament Index.* Rome: Biblical Institute Press, 1967.

Smolar, L. and M. Aberbach. *Studies in Targum Jonathan to the Prophets.* New York: Ktav, 1983; Baltimore: Hebrew College.

Sperber, A., ed. *The Bible in Aramaic Based on Old Manuscripts and Printed Texts.* 4 vols. Leiden: Brill, 1959-73.

*Vermes, G. *Scripture and Tradition in Judaism. Haggadic Studies.* 2nd rev. ed. Leiden: Brill, 1973.

York, A. D. "The Dating of Targumic Literature." *Journal for the Study of Judaism* 5 (1974) 49-62.

98
Synagogues

Brooten, B. *Women Leaders in the Ancient Synagogues. Inscriptional Evidence and Background Issues.* Chico: Scholars Press, 1982.

Chiat, M. S. *Handbook of Synagogue Architecture.* Chico: Scholars Press, 1982.

Gutmann, J. ed., *Ancient Synagogues. The State of Research.* Chico: Scholars Press, 1981.

Heinemann, J. *Prayer in the Talmud. Forms and Patterns.* Berlin—New York: de Gruyter. 1977.

*_____ and J. J. Petuchowski, eds. *Literature of the Synagogue. Edited with Introductions and Notes.* New York: Behrman House, 1975.

Hüttenmeister, F. and G. Reeg. *Die antiken Synagogen in Israel.* 2 vols. Wiesbaden—Dotzheim: L. Reichert, 1977.

Petuchowski, J. J., ed. *Contributions to the Scientific Study of Jewish Liturgy.* New York: Ktav, 1970.

Saller, S. J. *A Revised Catalogue of the Ancient Synagogues of the Holy Land.* Rev. ed. Jerusalem: Franciscan Printing Press, 1972.

99
Jewish Mysticism

Alexander, P. S. "Comparing Merkavah Mysticism and Gnosticism: An Essay in Method." *Journal of Jewish Studies* 35 (1984) 1-18.

Chernus, I. *Mysticism in Rabbinic Judaism. Studies in the History of Midrash.* Berlin—New York: de Gruyter, 1982.

Gruenwald, I. *Apocalyptic and Merkavah Mysticism.* Leiden—Cologne: Brill, 1980.

Halperin, D. J. *The Merkavah in Rabbinic Literature.* New Haven: American Oriental Society, 1980.

Schäfer, P. "Tradition and Redaction in Hekhalot Literature." *Journal for the Study of Judaism* 14 (1983) 172-81.

_____, ed. *Synopse zur Hekhalot-Literatur.* Tübingen: Mohr-Siebeck, 1981.

Scholem, G. *Jewish Gnosticism, Merkabah Mysticism and Talmudic Tradition.* New York: Schocken, 1965.

_____. *Major Trends in Jewish Mysticism.* 4th ed. New York: Schocken, 1969.

100
Early Christian History

*Bauer, W. *Orthodoxy and Heresy in Earliest Christianity.* Philadelphia: Fortress, 1971.

Benko, S. *Pagan Rome and the Early Christians.* Bloomington, IN: Indiana University Press, 1984.

Brown, R. E. and J. P. Meier. *Antioch and Rome. New Testament Cradles of Catholic Christianity.* New York-Ramsey, NJ: Paulist, 1983.

Bruce, F. F. *New Testament History.* Garden City, NY: Doubleday, 1972.

Conzelmann, H. *History of Primitive Christianity.* Nashville—New York: Abingdon, 1973.

Drijvers, H. J. W. "Facts and Problems in Early Syriac-Speaking Christianity." *Second Century* 2 (1982) 157-75.

Filson, F. V. *A New Testament History. The Story of the Emerging Church.* Philadelphia: Westminster, 1964.

Freyne, S. *The World of the New Testament.* Wilmington: Michael Glazier, 1980.

Grant, R. M. *Early Christianity and Society. Seven Studies.* New York—Hagerstown—San Francisco: Harper & Row, 1977.

Halton, T. P. and R. D. Sider. "A Decade of Patristic Scholarship 1970-1979." *Classical World* 76 (1982) 65-127, (1983) 313-83.

Hengel, M. *Between Jesus and Paul. Studies in the Earliest History of Christianity.* Philadelphia: Fortress, 1983.

*Lake, K., ed. *The Apostolic Fathers, with an English Translation* (1912). 2 vols. Cambridge, MA: Harvard University Press, 1970; London: Heinemann.

Leaney, A. R. C. *The Jewish and Christian World, 200 BC to AD 200.* Cambridge, UK—London—New York: Cambridge University Press, 1984.

Lightfoot, J. B., ed. *The Apostolic Fathers* (1891). Grand Rapids: Baker, 1983.

Lohse, E. *New Testament Environment.* Nashville: Abingdon, 1976.

MacMullen, R. *Christianizing the Roman Empire (A.D. 100-400).* New Haven—London: Yale University Press, 1984.

Malherbe, A. *Social Aspects of Early Christianity.* 2nd rev. ed. Philadelphia: Fortress, 1983.

Murray, R. *Symbols of Church and Kingdom. A Study in Early Syriac Tradition.* New York: Cambridge University Press, 1975.

*Osiek, C. *What Are They Saying About the Social Setting of the New Testament?* New York—Ramsey, NJ: Paulist, 1984.

Robinson, J. M. and H. Koester. *Trajectories through Early Christianity.* Philadelphia: Fortress, 1971.

Sanders, E. P., ed. *Jewish and Christian Self-Definition.* 3 vols. Philadelphia: Fortress, 1980-82.

Simon, M. "The *religionsgeschichtliche Schule*, fifty years later." *Religious Studies* 11 (1975) 135-44.

Sparks, J. N., ed. *The Apostolic Fathers.* Nashville—New York: Nelson, 1978.

Staniforth, M., ed. *Early Christian Writings. The Apostolic Fathers* (1968). Baltimore: Penguin, 1972.

Wilken, R. L. *The Christians as the Romans Saw Them.* New Haven—London: Yale University Press, 1984.

101
New Testament Apocrypha

Bovon, F., ed. *Les Actes apocryphes des apôtres. Christianisme et monde païen.* Geneva: Labor et Fides. 1981.

Cameron, R., ed. *The Other Gospels. Non-Canonical Gospel Texts.* Philadelphia: Westminster, 1982.

Crossan, J. D. *Four Other Gospels. Shadows on the Contours of Canon.* Minneapolis: Winston Press, 1985.

Davies, S. L. *The Revolt of the Widows. The Social World of the Apocryphal Acts.* Carbondale, IL: Southern Illinois University Press, 1980.

Grossi, V., ed. *Gli Apocrifi cristiani e cristianizzati.* Rome: Institutum Patristicum "Augustinianum," 1983.

*Hennecke, E., W. Schneemelcher, and R. McL. Wilson, eds. *New Testament Apocrypha.* 2 vols. Philadelphia: Westminster, 1963, 1966.

James, M. R. *The Apocryphal New Testament: Being the Apocryphal Gospels, Acts, Epistles and Apocalypses.* Oxford: Clarendon Press, 1953.

Jeremias, J. *Unknown Sayings of Jesus.* New York: Macmillan, 1957.

Koester, H. "Apocryphal and Canonical Gospels." *Harvard Theological Review* 73 (1980) 105-30.

Kraemer, R. S. "The Conversion of Women to Ascetic Forms of Christianity." *Signs* 6 (1980) 298-307.

Santos Otero, A. de., ed. *Los evangelios Apócrifos.* 3rd ed. Madrid: Edica, 1975.

102
Jewish Christianity

Daniélou, J. *The Theology of Jewish Christianity* (1964). Philadelphia: Westminster, 1977.

Klijn, A. F. J. "The Study of Jewish Christianity." *New Testament Studies* 20 (1974) 419-31.

*_____ and G. J. Reinink. *Patristic Evidence for Jewish-Christian Sects.* Leiden: Brill, 1973.

Malina, B. J. "Jewish Christianity or Christian Judaism: Toward a hypothetical Definition." *Journal for the Study of Judaism* 7 (1976) 46-57.

Manns, F. *Bibliographie du Judéo-Christianisme.* Jerusalem: Franciscan Printing Press, 1979.

Murray, R. "Defining Judaeo-Christianity." *Heythrop Journal* 15 (1974) 303-10.

Schoeps, H.—J. *Jewish Christianity. Factional Disputes in the Early Church.* Philadelphia: Fortress, 1969.

103
Gnosticism

Bianchi, U., ed. *Le origini dello gnosticismo. Colloquio di Messina.* 2 vols. Leiden: Brill, 1967.

Dart, J. *The Laughing Savior. The Discovery and Significance of the Nag Hammadi Gnostic Library.* New York—Hagerstown—San Francisco: Harper & Row, 1976.

The Facsimile Edition of the Nag Hammadi Codices. 12 vols. Leiden: Brill, 1972-79.

Foerster, W. and R. McL. Wilson, eds. *Gnosis. A Selection of Texts. I: Patristic Evidence; II: Coptic and Mandean Sources.* New York: Oxford University Press, 1972, 1974.

Green, H. A. "Gnosis and Gnosticism: A Study in Methodology." *Numen* 24 (1977) 95-134.

_____. "Suggested Sociological Themes in the Study of Gnosticism." *Vigiliae Christianae* 31 (1977) 169-80.

Jonas, H. *The Gnostic Religion. The Message of the Alien God and the Beginnings of Christianity.* Boston: Beacon, 1958.

Layton, B., ed. *The Rediscovery of Gnosticism.* 2 vols. Leiden: Brill, 1980-81.

Pagels, E. H. *The Gnostic Gospels.* New York: Random House, 1979.

Perkins, P. *The Gnostic Dialogue. The Early Church and the Crisis of Gnosticism.* New York—Ramsey, NJ—Toronto: Paulist, 1980.

*Robinson, J. M. *The Nag Hammadi Library in English*, New York—Hagerstown—San Francisco—London: Harper & Row, 1977.

*Rudolph, K. *Gnosis. The Nature and History of Gnosticism.* San Francisco: Harper & Row, 1983; Toronto: Fitzhenry & Whiteside.

Schenke, H.—M. "The Problem of Gnosis." *Second Century* 3 (1983) 73-87.

Scholer, D. M. *Nag Hammadi Bibliography 1948-1969; 1970-1982.* Leiden: Brill, 1971, 1985.

Tröger, K. W., ed. *Gnosis und Neues Testament. Studien aus Religionswissenschaft und Theologie.* Gütersloh: Mohn, 1973.

Wilson, R. McL. *The Gnostic Problem. A Study of the Relations Between Hellenistic Judaism and the Gnostic Problem.* 2nd ed. London: Mowbray, 1964.

_____. "'Jewish Gnosis' and Gnostic Origins: A Survey." *Hebrew Union College Annual* 45 (1974) 177-89.

_____. "Nag Hammadi and the New Testament." *New Testament Studies* 28 (1982) 289-302.

Yamauchi, E. M. *Pre-Christian Gnosticism. A Survey of Proposed Evidences.* 2nd ed. Grand Rapids: Baker, 1983.

INDEX OF NAMES